Praise for *Sprocket* and Stephanie Novak Hau

helps keep them naturally engaged in the work. As someone who researches and focuses on organizational management, I can personally attest to the impact the Sprocket framework has had on organizations in growth mode as well as those that are more stable and mature. *Sprocket* challenges existing mindsets, creates breakthrough moments, and helps organizations establish and/or sustain a competitive advantage."

—Kristi Weierbach, PhD
Organizational Management

"*Sprocket* provides an honest, personalized perspective to evolve your business with built-in buy-in at all levels through transparent communication. Your leadership and team members will engage in the initiative and help you bring about necessary change, allowing your organization to grow and thrive. It's a brilliant and refreshing approach for leaders of all business types and sizes. And as the new generation of workers continues to enter the workforce with unique skills, abilities, and beliefs, *Sprocket* helps create an inclusive environment ripe for innovation and success."

—Teri O'Neal
Associate Vice President, University Communications, Towson University

"We applied the Sprocket approach to better serve our students. Sprocket transformed our team from hard working to high achieving. The methodology was clear, and the results were compelling. It will serve as our leadership playbook moving forward."

—Stephen DiBiagio, MBA, MEd
President, The John Carroll School

"Successful business leaders understand three things about change: it *is* coming, it will be unsettling, and it will present new opportunities. In *Sprocket*, Stephanie Hau helps organizations prepare for change by offering a unique and logical approach to strategic planning. Her scientific analysis of the key components of a resilient business design brings renewed meaning to concepts like culture and purpose. Stephanie uses simple equations to demonstrate the interdependence of these design components and shows that failing to adequately cultivate any one of these components will inevitably cause an imbalance in the equation, potentially resulting in an ineffective plan. She also dispels many of the traditional (and tired) strategic planning myths, encouraging us to focus instead on what inspires employees and customers. *Sprocket* offers an innovative road map to organizations facing contemporary challenges. It is an essential tool for all thoughtful leaders."

–Michael Allen
President, Harford Bank

Sprocket

Sprocket

THE MECHANICS OF BUSINESS SUCCESS

Stephanie
Novak Hau

Advantage | Books

Published by Advantage Books, Charleston, South Carolina.
An imprint of Advantage Media.

ADVANTAGE is a registered trademark, and the Advantage colophon is a trademark of Advantage Media Group, Inc.

Printed in the United States of America.

10 9 8 7 6 5 4 3 2 1

ISBN: 978-1-64225-959-9 (Paperback)
ISBN: 978-1-64225-958-2 (eBook)

Library of Congress Control Number: 2024901762

Cover and layout design by Matthew Morse.

This publication is designed to provide accurate and authoritative information in regard to the subject matter covered. It is sold with the understanding that the publisher is not engaged in rendering legal, accounting, or other professional services. If legal advice or other expert assistance is required, the services of a competent professional person should be sought.

Advantage Books is an imprint of Advantage Media Group. Advantage Media helps busy entrepreneurs, CEOs, and leaders write and publish a book to grow their business and become the authority in their field. Advantage authors comprise an exclusive community of industry professionals, idea-makers, and thought leaders. For more information go to **advantagemedia.com**.

This book is dedicated to my sons, Jack and Alex,
who inspire me every day to do things of lasting value.

Contents

PART 3

Optimizing the Sprocket Design

Foreword

After ten years of booming business, our landscape architecture firm had grown to a team of thirty-plus people across two cities. We had organically organized ourselves into two teams to manage a growing number of projects and deadlines. There was nothing inherently unique about these teams—we'd simply split the firm in half and assigned projects based on availability. It didn't take long to see that this loosely defined structure was not as effective as we needed it to be! Our leadership team spent several months developing a new structure based on internal roles and responsibilities. Before implementing the new structure, we reached out to our business consultant to validate that we were approaching the restructuring correctly. That's when we were introduced to Stephanie and the Sprocket Assessment.

Over the following months, the Sprocket Assessment challenged our leadership group to change our thinking about how our business operates at a fundamental level. The easy-to-complete surveys revealed that our team was clear on our business purpose but that we were much less clear on strategy, processes, and, of course, structure.

Our first step with Stephanie was to develop a purpose statement that resonated with our team. Compared to previous statements, the phrase we landed on is clear, concise, and memorable. It is now used in all of our marketing materials, and our staff knows this phrase by heart.

Using the newly defined purpose statement as a basis, we dissected our business strategy using the Sprocket Strategy Assessment. We analyzed existing data to understand profitability and win rates. We also polled our staff to learn what type of work they are passionate about and what client groups they enjoy working with. This deep dive helped us formulate a clear business strategy based on the type of clients that would both benefit from and support our firm's purpose. We identified six client groups who fit this description and established portfolio targets for each. This gave our marketing team a measurable goal for future business development efforts.

The biggest transformation came from the Sprocket Structure Assessment. Based on the new client type targets, we completely changed our internal structure to maximize value for our clients. It was challenging to think about restructuring the firm based on our clients and not on the internal mechanics of delivering a project. The thorough explanations provided in the Sprocket Assessment helped us to make this transition, and we now have three unique teams that are dedicated to serving specific client types. Organizing by client type has allowed our staff to develop expertise and deepen professional relationships. We are also excited that our younger team members retained the ability to experience a wide range of project types, no matter which client team they are a part of.

The Sprocket Assessment has fundamentally shifted our company from being driven by internal factors to being 100 percent focused on the most critical element of our business: our clients. Our team is excited to have clarity on their growth potential within the firm, and our clients are benefiting from focused expertise serving their projects. The work of running a business is never finished, but we now have a solid framework to help guide our decision-making moving forward, thanks to Stephanie and the Sprocket Model!

—Mindy Cooper, PLA

Principal, dwg
December 2023

Introduction

Adapt or die.

Charles Darwin[1] wasn't that direct when he proposed his ground-breaking theory of evolution, but his meaning was clear. Organisms that successfully adapt to changes in their environment survive, and those that don't die, extinction becoming the ultimate fate of their species.

As a business leader, you know this is your reality, too. When businesses fail to adapt to changes in their environment, performance suffers. If ineffective adaptation is allowed to persist, poor performance progresses first to obsolescence and then ultimately to failure. The failure will be incorrectly chalked up to external forces that were out of the business's control. In reality, the failure resulted from an inability to effectively respond to these forces, which was well within the business's control.

In the natural world, changes and the resulting necessary adaptive responses required by organisms generally take place over decades, centuries, or millennia. Consider that the earth's major landforms are

---

1   Charles Darwin and Leonard Kebler, *On the Origin of Species by Means of Natural Selection, or, the Preservation of Favoured Races in the Struggle for Life* (London: John Murray, 1859).

created and destroyed by tectonic plates that move less than one inch per year. Even when catastrophic events occur (a volcano erupts or an asteroid hits the earth), changing landforms instantly, it can take years to fully realize their impacts on organisms.

In the business world, change occurs at such a fast and furious pace that you are lucky if you have days to adapt, let alone years.

In 1900, the world was only just beginning to harness the power of electricity and the combustion engine. At that time in history, it took *one hundred years* for the totality of human knowledge to double.[2] In the ensuing century, the world experienced an explosion of technological innovations, including (and this is the short list) aviation, television, nuclear power, computers, and the internet—with human knowledge doubling *every twelve months* and predictions that it would soon be *every twelve hours!*[3]

Change in the world is so rapid, so widespread, and so constant that it can feel at times like it is impossible to keep up. The world is yelling "Faster!" while businesses are still slowing down to negotiate the hazards in the road that the last change created. We are witnesses to the exponential nature of change—the more it occurs, the faster it occurs.

The degree to which your organization can implement appropriate adaptive responses to change is dependent on its effectiveness and efficiency. *Effectiveness* is the ability to produce a better result, one that delivers more value. *Efficiency* is the ability to create and deliver this value using the least amount of time, effort, and resources.

If your organization is like most, your business design is compromising its effectiveness and efficiency. When change occurs, the

---

2   R. Buckminster Fuller, *Critical Path*, 1st ed. (New York: St. Martin's Press, 1981).

3   David Russell Schilling, "Knowledge doubling every 12 months, soon to be every 12 hours," IndustryTap.com, April 19, 2013, accessed December 2023, https://www.industrytap.com/knowledge-doubling-every-12-months-soon-to-be-every-12-hours/3950.

degree to which your organization is ineffective and inefficient will determine how well (or even if) it can implement an appropriate adaptive response. If you want your organization to thrive and not just survive (or even dive), you need a better design—one that will allow you to identify and implement transformational changes without major interruptions to operations.

Right now, it's trendy to try to anticipate and prepare for all the changes coming your way. Doesn't it make more sense to own a vehicle that allows you to drive your business forward, whether conditions are sunny and clear or dark and stormy, and nimbly adjust to changing road conditions without sliding into a ditch or plunging over a cliff (even if you *can't* see any pavement markers or road signs telling you what's up ahead)?

This book introduces you to a better design for your business that I call Sprocket. Adopting this more intentional design will allow you to optimize your organization to run effectively and efficiently and adapt quickly and successfully to changes in your business landscape so that you are not stuck on the side of the road with all your competitors.

As a *scientist*, I am educated and experienced in performing detailed research to further the body of knowledge in a given field by observing phenomena, devising hypotheses that explain these phenomena, and designing experiments and/or collecting additional data to test those hypotheses. This approach is an iterative process, meaning it's a cycle rather than a straight line. The more times the cycle is repeated, the better the answers get through the process of convergence. As an *applied scientist*, my work starts with acquiring knowledge, but my endgame is applying this knowledge to design and build practical solutions to real-world problems.

Our modern society, particularly in the business world, puts a premium on being smart. But being smart is no substitute for having knowledge, and having knowledge is no substitute for acting. If you only take one lesson away from reading this book, let it be this one.

In my more than thirty years as a business owner, I have worked with hundreds of clients representing small private organizations (less than ten employees); large private organizations (thousands of employees); local, state, and federal agencies; and nonprofit entities of all sizes. This work led me to discover that there are five critical components that drive up effectiveness, efficiency, and accountability in organizations, helping them to succeed over the long term by allowing them to adapt to changes without significant disruption to their operations.

This work also uncovered another pattern that I was not expecting. The business leaders I interacted with were almost without exception aware of the problems with effectiveness, efficiency, and accountability in their organizations, but saw them as by and large unavoidable, much like death and taxes.

When their organizations were strained due to events such as acquisitions, market fluctuations, or regulatory changes, they mistakenly viewed the negative impacts on their operations to be the result of these external forces *only*. They did not understand or appreciate that these external forces were merely accentuating their existing problems with effectiveness, efficiency, and accountability. That's analogous to getting into a car accident and blaming wet roads when the tires were bald and the brakes were shot.

If you are a business leader struggling with low levels of effectiveness, efficiency, and accountability, this book will help you understand the underlying causes, what needs to change, and how to affect that change with limited angst so that you can successfully adapt when external forces change your business landscape—again. I've divided this book into three parts to explain where you are now, where you need to be, and how to get there.

Part 1:

○ Illustrates and explains the outdated design under which your business is operating and why it is wholly inadequate for creating effective and efficient organizations today

○ Explains how this design will ultimately doom your business because of the three forces that are currently reshaping the business landscape and will be for the foreseeable future

Part 2:

○ Introduces a more intentional design that incorporates the five critical components that are needed to achieve high levels of efficiency, effectiveness, and accountability

○ Explains how these critical components work together as a system so that you understand how to create more synergies and less interferences among them

Part 3:

○ Teaches you the most effective method to implement transformational change in your organization

○ Provides a "blueprint" with step-by-step instructions of how to build the best version of each of these critical components so that you can minimize disruptions to your operations during periods of required change

I have seen the impact this design has had on organizations where it has been applied. After years of frustration trying to *pull* the door open, their leaders learned how a slight *push* was all that was needed.

My purpose in writing this book is to share my findings with you so that you can put this knowledge to work in your organization, making it more effective, more efficient, and more responsive to change—regardless of whether the market is up or down, the economy is growing or shrinking, or who is sitting behind the "big desk."

When change comes, and it will, you don't want to be in the driver's seat of a Model T or Pinto.

Are you ready to embark on a journey together to drive your business forward, watching all the inefficiencies and misdirection and confusion get smaller and smaller in the rearview mirror? If so, what are we waiting for? Let's get started!

**Design is not just
what it looks like and feels like.
Design is how it works.**

STEVE JOBS

PART 1

The Inherited Business Design

Causes Your Business to Misfire

If you're a leader in an organization, your biggest frustration is likely how hard it is to move the needle in the areas of effectiveness, efficiency, and accountability. Since these are measures of employee behaviors, you might logically conclude that resolving these issues is a matter of fixing your people or "culture" (our latest ill-defined business buzzword). It may be logical, but it is incorrect.

The problem is not your people; it's your business design. The harsh reality is that today's business design is a composite response to past business sensibilities and, therefore, is wholly inadequate to meet the present needs of customers and employees, even under the best of circumstances. When stressors are applied to the business in the form of substantive changes in the economy, the market, or the regulatory environment, this legacy design can and does doom a business.

Let's explore the origin of this business design you inherited; how it's negatively impacting effectiveness, efficiency, and accountability in your organization; and how it's making your business more vulnerable to threats.

What's Around the Bend

In chapter 1, we'll explore the four outdated and ineffective components of the inherited business design by defining them and investigating their individual impact on the effectiveness, efficiency, accountability, and adaptability of a business.

In chapter 2, we'll explore the three major forces that are straining that legacy business design to a breaking point.

Let's get our journey started.

**If I had asked my customers
what they wanted,
they would have said a faster horse.**

———

HENRY FORD

CHAPTER 1

Its Obsolescent Components

Organizational Charts, Mission/Vision
Statements, Value Propositions, Money Focus

When I ask business leaders what their business architecture looks like, I generally get a quizzical look, followed by "You mean our organizational chart?"

Every business operates under the guidance of an organizational chart. But have you ever considered whether this tool helps to drive up effectiveness, efficiency, and accountability in your organization, or whether it helps you to quickly and successfully implement adaptive responses to changes in your business landscape?

Organizational Charts: A Graphical Directory of the Big Dogs

A little history. The first organizational chart ever produced was by the Tabulating Machine Company, which was truly groundbreaking—in 1917!

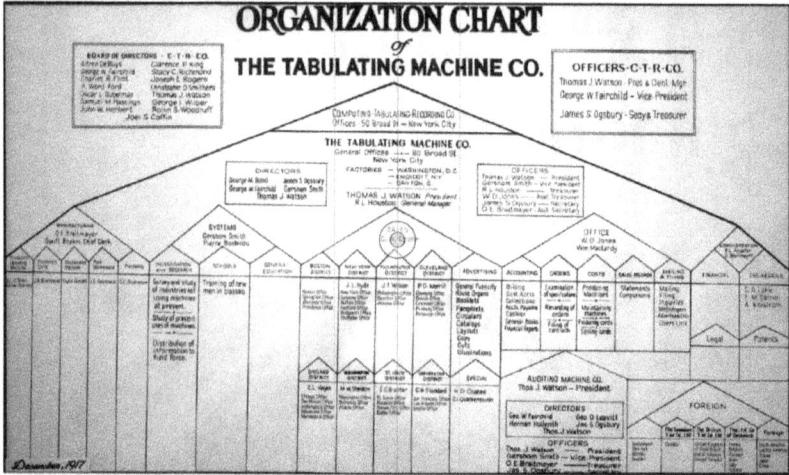

Figure 1.1

I am going to go out on a limb here and guess that the organizational chart you use in your business looks very much the same. The names and fonts are different, of course, and yours was probably generated using software, but the sum and substance remains the same.

And what is this organizational chart meant to convey?

First and foremost, it is meant to convey the *hierarchy* of the organization, where people or groups are ranked one above the other according to status or authority. In other words, a nice graphic to depict everyone in the business. Well, not everyone, just the important and powerful. And since the business world has been using this tool for more than a century, we keep inventing new titles for the important and powerful. You know, to keep it fresh.

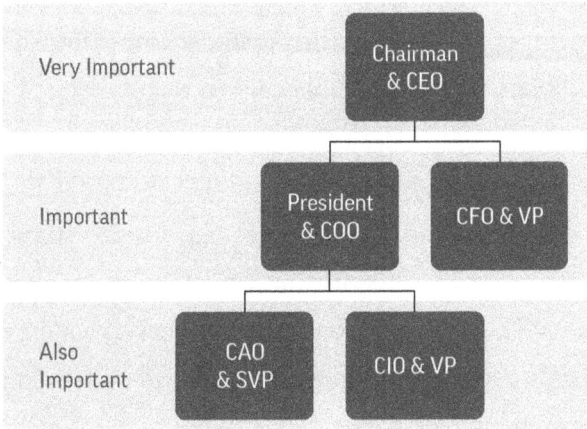

Figure 1.2

"Frank, what does Rachel do?"

"She's in information and reports to Jim."

"Information? I thought the 'I' in CIO stood for innovation?"

"No, I'm pretty sure it's information."

"Well, what does she do in information?"

"She reports to Jim."

"Well, what does Jim do?"

"I think he's a VP."

"Does he run the department?"

"No, I think you have to be a senior VP to run a department."

"Oh. I thought senior VPs just owned more stock than VPs."

In addition to your organizational chart not helping your employees to understand how your business is organized—and why—it is actually hurting their morale and engagement. Whether intentional or not, these charts tell your employees that your business operates under an Us/Them model, where the important, powerful, and *visible* people (Us) oversee the work of the unimportant, powerless, and *invisible* people in the organization (Them). This might (might!) have been acceptable in 1917 when workers were universally considered to be dispensable, replaceable cogs in the machine. But do you really believe that the majority of your employees who do not see their name on your organizational chart are OK with being invisible, seemingly dispensable and replaceable? No, I didn't think so. More to the point, how can your organizational chart possibly drive up effectiveness, efficiency, and accountability of everyone in your organization if only your leaders are represented and even then in a vague and confusing framework?

While the organizational chart *may* have served a useful purpose initially, I think it's fair to say that this hierarchical approach, which ascribes zero value or autonomy to the *majority of employees* working in a business, has outlived its usefulness. Its major flaw is that it focuses on the "who" and not the "what" or the "why" of your structure. Continuing to use an organizational chart is the epitome of the "But that's the way we've always done it" mentality. The world has changed enormously since 1917, and your business design needs to reflect those changes.

Second, an organizational chart suggests that each vertical in the diagram functions independently from the other verticals under the watchful eye of its assigned leader. If departments are run as separate silos, how well can the business respond to substantive changes in the economy, market, or regulatory arena requiring a systemic response? Will leadership be able to define and deploy responses that help the employees throughout the organization quickly and successfully adapt so that they can continue to work effectively and efficiently with minimal interruption? In other words, does this design make the business more or less resilient to threats? Let's take a look.

When a business is designed and operated as a set of independent departments or silos, and significant forces act upon the organization as a whole, debates invariably occur about which subjective perspective should be implemented to respond. Managers focus myopically on the operations of their department or sphere of influence, with little regard for other departments.

This is what I call the Rubik's Cube management response. The Blue Department manager, for example, deploys initiatives in response to the forces acting on the business that are perceived to be impacting the Blue Department. At the same time, the Red Department manager deploys a separate set of initiatives that are somewhat in conflict with those of the Blue Department to respond to perceived impacts to the Red Department. As soon as the Green Department manager hears about these initiatives, they fire off multiple emails in response, outlining how these initiatives will negatively impact the Green Department. Meanwhile, the poor Orange Department manager is occupied with responding to the changes initiated by the Blue and Red Department managers, completely unaware that those initiatives are currently being modified per the response by the Green Department manager.

One side of the cube gets solved; another side gets disrupted. The business struggles mightily as these independent responses to the forces acting on it compete with one another. What was previously a high-functioning organization is now floundering as it tries unsuccessfully to minimize the disruption to its workforce. Neither the managers nor the CEO understands why this is happening, because everyone seems to be "working on the problem."

If you are leading a business using this siloed design, your ability to successfully adapt to changes with minimal interruptions to production is slim to none, and to quote the late, great Muhammad Ali, "Slim just left town."

Mission/Vision Statements: The Dreaded Writing Assignment

Type "worst mission statements" into your search bar, and you'll get thirty-five million results! If you've ever written a mission statement, this probably doesn't surprise you.

Why do so many of us dread writing mission/vision statements, and why do they end up being so terrible despite our best efforts? For starters, universally accepted definitions for these terms do not exist, which is standard fare for trendy business buzzwords. Some define missions as what the business "does" and visions as what the business "wants to be." Others define missions as the "what" of the business and visions as the "why." And still others define missions as the "today" of the business and visions as its "tomorrow." As Charlie Brown would say, "Good Grief!"

Mission and vision statements became popular in the 1980s as a means of humanizing businesses. As you now understand, this was needed because organizational charts are dehumanizing.

These vague and confusing messages make it impossible for most of us to truly understand what our mission and vision statements are meant to accomplish. It's no wonder most of us hate writing them. And even after a large investment of time and effort to craft these statements and plaster them on internal and external websites, employees can rarely recite these supposed "guiding lights" of the organization they work for.

And yet, no matter where you look, you cannot escape the collective rallying cry in the business world that every business absolutely must have both a mission *and* vision statement to be successful. So, the obvious question is, "If we don't understand what 'vision' and 'mission' mean, or what the vision or mission statement is meant to accomplish, how are these statements helping our people to perform their jobs effectively and efficiently?" They're not. If your employees can't even remember these statements, you can be certain that they are not functioning as a guiding light for the work being performed in your organization.

Value Propositions: How to Telegraph Sameness

Honest. Qualified. Experienced. Expert. Capable.

What do these words have in common? They all convey the same thing: a standard benchmark for competency that all customers expect from any business. And yet, these are exactly the kinds of words we have been taught since the 1990s to use in our value proposition—a statement that purportedly tells potential customers why they should do business with us and not our competitors.

But if every company in a given industry is using similar words in their value proposition, are potential customers really being given a strong argument for doing business with one company over another? The answer, of course, is no.

And yet the collective business world stubbornly holds on to the false notion that a business must have a *value proposition* to capture more market share. Here's the reality. Because you and your competitors use similar words to explain your value, you actually reinforce the belief by customers that there is *no significant difference* between you and your competitors. Value propositions don't communicate uniqueness, they communicate sameness. That's not helpful.

Money Focus: A Limiting Measure of Performance

In my experience, businesses operating under the inherited, outdated business design all too often have a singular money focus when assessing performance. And, by a money focus, I mean that performance is *only* measured and considered through a lens of monetary value. How much did we earn this quarter/fiscal year? How much was our profit? What can we give our employees as a bonus? What is the dividend payout to stockholders? How much can we sell our stock for? How much can we sell the company for? Basically, how much money is the business making and who gets it?

Of course, measuring your financial performance is a critical responsibility of you as a leader in your organization, but if that is *all* you look at, you lose the opportunity to assess the behavior, capabilities, and operational environment of your people, which is analogous to bragging about how fast that sports coupe in your garage can go. As we explore the alternative business design that I recommend you to adopt, I'll show you how adding a people focus will make your business stronger and more resilient than a singular money focus. You'll brag not only about how many miles you get to the gallon but also about how comfortable the ride is for your passengers.

> Issues with accountability, effectiveness, and efficiency in a business are not caused by its people but by its design.

What's Around the Bend

And there you have it. Today's business design is nothing more than an inherited composite of elements created to meet business sensibilities of yesteryear. There is an organizational chart (circa 1900s), a mission and/or vision statement (circa 1980s), and a value proposition (circa 1990s). Do you think the business world is due for an upgrade? I certainly do.

In part 2, I'll show you a more effective alternative to:

- ⚙ the standard organizational chart that will help your employees understand how all departments function; will drive up effectiveness, efficiency, and accountability; and will facilitate successful adaptive responses to changes while putting the final nail in the coffin of the antiquated and dehumanizing Us/Them message.

- ⚙ mission/vision statements that convey the true purpose of your business, allowing them to attract enthusiastic customers and employees like a giant magnet, committing them to a cause that they believe provides true value.

- ⚙ value propositions that will truly set you apart in the minds of your customers because they are as unique as fingerprints, so cannot be appropriated by your competition.

But before we get to that, we need to discuss three major stressors facing all businesses today—stressors that can cripple *your* business if you do not intentionally account for them in your design.

The only constant in life is change.

GREEK PHILOSOPHER
HERACLITUS

CHAPTER 2

Major Forces
Straining This Design

Emerging Technology, People Preferences,
Market Consolidation/Fragmentation

As we discussed in chapter 1, an optimal business design maximizes effectiveness, efficiency, and accountability, allowing the people in the business to implement adaptive responses to changes in the environment with minimal interruptions to operations. Fortunately, many of the changes that will occur in your business environment will be either insignificant or a one-off, so implementing an adaptive response without large-scale disruptions to operations will be fairly straightforward even if your levels of effectiveness, efficiency, and accountability are not particularly high. For example, if a key manager is late to work because they ran out of gas or got a flat because their tires were under-inflated, someone else could assume the manager's responsibilities for the short term with only minor disruptions to operations.

But there are three external forces acting on your business—emerging technology, people preferences, and market consolidation/

fragmentation—that, because they are both significant and perpetual, will cause any business with low levels of effectiveness, efficiency, and accountability to struggle with adaptive responses without significant interruptions to its operations. For example, if your business is located in an area that is prone to seasonal wildfires or hurricanes, large-scale disruptions to operations during and after these catastrophic events could only be avoided by having a comprehensive and field-tested disaster response plan that identifies alternate work locations, provides instruction on how to access and use remote work technologies, and outlines a company-wide communications plan. The development, maintenance, and successful implementation of such a plan would require high levels of effectiveness, efficiency, and accountability throughout the organization.

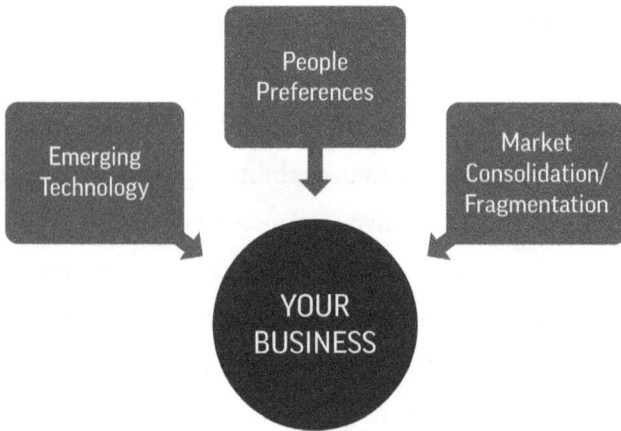

Figure 2.1

Let's explore how each of these pernicious forces is straining your organization. Better buckle up because it's going to be a bumpy ride.

Emerging Technology: Every Coin Has Two Sides

Every new technology is introduced with great fanfare about how it will make our lives better. This is the promise. We can argue about whether technology does, in fact, make our lives better, but there can be no disagreement that it makes our lives faster. This is the reality. And that speeding up of our lives has a very real downside. If you are not diligent and deliberate, the rapid influx of new technologies, and the continuing "improvements" to existing technologies, can steamroll your operations.

INFORMATION OVERLOAD: THE BEST WAY TO STIFLE DECISION-MAKING

Me: "Where's Angela?"

Ramon: "In Vietnam for the next three weeks."

Me: "How do I reach her?"

Ramon: "You can't. She is off-grid for the next month."

Me: "She can't be off-grid—I need to get my hands on the comments from our client on the latest wetlands report for US 301, and I need it now!"

Ramon: "I can get in her email, give me a sec. … Alright, I'm in. I see her US 301 email folder. When did the client send back comments? She has 250 stored emails here, so I'll need to sort by date."

Me: "Um … maybe last April or May."

Ramon turned his chair around to face me. "Great! That narrows it down to 227 emails to look at. Can't we just ask the client?"

Me: "No. They are adamant that the comments they just sent were previously sent and never addressed. We know that we addressed the previous comments, and they sent an email accepting our revisions. These are new comments, and unless we find that email, we'll have to address them for free."

We could not locate the email with proof that we addressed all comments to the satisfaction of the client. This resulted in our having to address new comments without charging our time. Yup, this employee's failure to document critical project communications in our enterprise software cost our company $20,000 in lost revenue.

Anyone who tries to justify hoarding thousands of emails by claiming that their "system" allows them to find any important email is lying or delusional. Yes, that means you. Excessive and unorganized emails (meaning only you understand the organizational scheme), frequent software upgrades, and the compulsion to always be online are each contributing to a reduction in employee effectiveness at an alarming rate. Taken in combination, they are further reducing effectiveness by degrading the decision-making skills of employees through the phenomenon of "information overload."

The concept of information overload was made popular by Alvin Toffler,[4] who defined it as an excessive quantity of information resulting in poor decision-making. This phenomenon was already observed to be having a significant impact in 1970, when the only means of acquiring new information was through print media, television, and radio!

---

4   Alvin Toffler, *Future Shock* (New York: Random House, 1970).

It's safe to assume that the impacts of information overload have exponentially increased over the last fifty-plus years, courtesy of the internet. Now, we call this phenomenon "busy brain." Different name, same negative impact.

According to Joseph Ruff of the Learning Innovations Laboratories of the Harvard Graduate School of Education, information overload has long been a concern for professional workers, for whom having too much information is analogous to having too little:[5]

> As might be expected, with little or no information, individuals have little or nothing to process and consequently make poor decisions. As the amount of information increases, so too does information processing and the quality of decision-making. However, after a certain point is reached, the decision-maker has obtained more information than he can process, information overload has occurred, and decision-making ability decreases. Any information received beyond that point will not be processed, may lead to confusion, and could have a negative impact on the individual's ability to set priorities as well as remember previous information.

The following phenomena and their degree of severity are good indicators of how prevalent information overload is in your organization. Here are just a few examples of the causes and impacts of information overload that Ruff identifies:[6]

---

5   Joseph Ruff, "Information Overload: Causes, Symptoms, and Solutions," December 2002, accessed October 2023, https://workplacepsychology.files.wordpress. com/2011/05/information_overload_causes_symptoms_and_solutions_ruff.pdf.

6   Ibid.

Causes of Information Overload in Business Settings

- Introduction of more technology than needed; poor integration of technologies used
- Lack of procedures and confusion as to the best practices for completing tasks
- Disembodied training and knowledge management departments
- Reliance on individual "heroes" who make the decisions and do the work

Impacts of Information Overload in Business Settings

- Poor concentration due to the overloading of short-term memory
- Multitasking resulting in diminished rather than increased productivity
- Belief that one must constantly rush to keep pace ("hurry sickness")
- Compulsion to check email, voicemail, and all things online to stay in "touch"

There is an idea gaining popularity in the world of psychology that trauma does not necessarily result from an event but from any situation that overloads our coping skills.[7] If information overload is effectively overwhelming our coping skills, then the rising rates of ADHD, anxiety, and depression among our population, especially among our digital-native youths, begin to make sense. As these young

---

7   Mary C. Lamia, "Strain trauma: When prolonged stress is just too much," August 23, 2020, accessed October 2023, https://www.psychology-today.com/us/blog/intense-emotions-and-strong-feelings/202008/strain-trauma-when-prolonged-stress-is-just-too.

people join the workforce, the impact on businesses will be substantial and predictable.

I was shopping at my local grocery store not too long ago when I noticed an older man staring at a section of shelving as I walked down the aisle toward him. He looked exasperated, so I offered help. Me: "Do you need help finding something?"

Him: "I can't find the canned sliced tomatoes. My wife asked me to stop at the store on my way home and pick up a few things. This is the only item I can't find, and I have been looking and looking."

Me: "Did you say canned *sliced* tomatoes?"

Him: "Yeah."

Me: "Are you sure she said sliced and not diced?"

Him: "I'm pretty sure she said sliced."

Me: "I've never seen canned sliced tomatoes. You can get diced tomatoes in a can. But, if you are sure that she wanted sliced tomatoes, you'll need to go to the produce section. Do you know what she is making?"

Him: "Dinner. I better get both kinds just in case!"

He thanked me profusely and threw a few cans each of regular, fire-roasted, garlic, basil, and low-sodium diced tomatoes into his cart and then rushed off to the produce section. I didn't have the heart to tell him that he'd have to choose between cherry, grape, hot house, local, and on the vine varieties.

Information overload!

EMAIL: YOUR NEVER-ENDING TO-DO LIST

Three hundred billion emails are sent each day. Less than eight billion people inhabit the planet. You do the math.

A twelve-year study of CEO habits conducted by the *Harvard Business Review* indicated that CEOs are spending 24 percent of their working hours looking at and responding to emails, even though they found it to interrupt their work and extend their workday, and it was not conducive to thoughtful discussions. In addition, they felt pressure to respond to FYI emails on which they were copied to avoid seeming rude.[8]

Studies published by Gloria Mark of the University of California, Irvine, found that it takes an average of twenty-five minutes to return to an original task after an interruption. This means that you (and your employees) are at least losing twenty-five minutes of productivity every time you stop what you're doing to read email, more if you count the time spent reading and responding to the email![9] And, you wonder why at the end of another long workday you feel like you got nothing accomplished.

I think we can all agree that the email anecdote I shared at the beginning of this section is, unfortunately, something most of us can relate to. Why? Because we simply can't process the flood of emails that inundates us daily. So, what's the big deal about storing boatloads of emails? I'll skip the debate about how email impacts the planet

---

8   Myelle Lansat, "An analysis of CEOs' schedules scrutinized 60,000 hours and found email is an even bigger time sink than people realize," BusinessInsider. com, June 28, 2018, accessed October 2023, https://www.businessinsider.com/ email-dangerous-time-sink-for-ceos-study-2018-6.

9   Bob Sullivan and Hugh Thompson, "Opinion: Brain, interrupted," The New York Times, May 3, 2013, accessed October 2023, https://www.nytimes.com/2013/05/05/ opinion/sunday/a-focus-on-distraction.html.

(reduces paper pollution but increases carbon emissions) and focus on impacts on people.

Ever heard of the Zeigarnik effect? The Zeigarnik effect states that people remember unfinished or interrupted tasks better than they remember completed tasks. That means that every uncompleted task is stored in the brain like a car alarm that no one deactivates. And, just like that horn that won't stop beeping, the memory of the uncompleted task causes a stress response. Who hasn't had the experience of lying awake at night feeling anxious about an unfinished task?

The email inbox is nothing more than the modern version of the old paper to-do list. Except, the old to-do list was created by *you*, usually on a small piece of paper, and once you completed a task, you had a sense of gratification, accomplishment, and relief as you crossed it off your list.

Today's to-do list is no longer created by you. It's created by anyone with access to your email address. To make matters worse, senders can and do flag their emails as having "High Importance," insist on adding "Read Receipts" to know exactly when you read their email, and even tell you when they expect follow-up (today, tomorrow, now!). With this daily inundation, it's impossible to respond to every email, and your "busy brain" ensures that the ones you do respond to contain responses or decisions that do not reflect your best thinking.

To formulate a well-thought-out and intelligent response, we need time to process information being provided and understand questions being asked. When our brain is working to reply, reply, reply as fast as we can, there is not adequate time for that processing and understanding to occur. But to stop the reply, reply, reply mindset would feel like insanity, because for every five emails we reply to, ten new ones show up in our inbox. Time and tide and emails wait for no man.

Every time you get a notification of a new email (PSA: turn that feature off) or glance at your inbox, the Zeigarnik effect is operating, increasing your stress levels as your brain receives the command that these "tasks" must be remembered until completed. But you cannot possibly remember them all.

Past forms of communicating tasks provided us with adequate time between receiving a request and making an appropriate response. For instance, I was cleaning out my mother's papers some years ago and came across a file she created when my father died in 1972. I opened more than a few envelopes from various attorneys that had the same typed letter inside:

> Dear Mrs. Novak,
> Please call this office upon receipt of this letter.
> Sincerely,
> (Name of Attorney)

That was it—nothing more.

Since there were no email, voicemail, or answering machines in 1972, the only way you could get in touch with someone was by calling them on the telephone and hoping they answered or sending a letter through the US Postal Service. Can you imagine how the attorney's message to my mother would play out today? Multiple emails per week, if not per day, that would read something like this:

> Mrs. Novak—Please read the seven documents I have attached and get back to me with how you would like to proceed by COB tomorrow. BTW, Form 1248 is critical!! Thanks.

I am going to guess that just reading that *fake* email caused you to have a very *real* stress reaction!

To recap, we are:

- ⚙ receiving more emails than we can possibly read,
- ⚙ spending a significant number of working hours responding to them,
- ⚙ feeling pressure to respond to them immediately, and
- ⚙ storing in the thousands the ones we don't have time to process.

This leads to:

- ⚙ poor decision-making,
- ⚙ significant decrease in productivity, and
- ⚙ undue stress that is negatively impacting our physical and mental health.

SOFTWARE UPDATES: THE GIFT THAT JUST KEEPS TAKING

"How's the new project going?"

"It's not."

"What? It got pulled?"

"Oh no, it's supposed to be happening right now, but we had another forced software update, and halfway through the update, the system crashed. I've been on hold with tech support for the last two hours while trying to manually piecemeal the project report that's due this afternoon."

"Good luck with that. I hope you can resolve it by end of day today."

"And then we can start updating everyone on the update …"

Employees today are spending a disproportionate amount of time learning new software or new versions of software. Even simple word processing software can keep employees on a chronically steep learning curve as new versions and updates are released in a never-ending cycle. More complex software, particularly those that must rapidly respond to changes in laws and regulations, such as for accounting or human resources, robs even more time from employees that could have been used to increase their knowledge and expertise in their chosen field, making them less valuable to their organizations.

To put into perspective how quickly things are changing and how those rapid changes impact efficiency today, let's consider what used to be a ubiquitous piece of office equipment. The typewriter was patented in 1878 and introduced the world to the QWERTY key layout. For more than a hundred years, the only significant changes made to this machine were the addition of electricity and correction tape (which I very much appreciated during my college years). Since there was nothing new to learn, typists could focus on increasing their proficiency as measured in their "words per minute." Contrast that with a word processor who had to relearn and remaster software thirty-five times between 1980 and 2020. Today and tomorrow's employees will become increasingly less proficient in their jobs, because the software they must use will change with jarring frequency throughout their career, and no matter how minor the update, new learning will be required, and that is an unwanted time suck.

There goes your efficiency.

People Preferences: Stop Making It a Generational Thing

According to the *Harvard Business Review*, today's employees want their jobs to not only meet their expectations for compensation and benefits, but they also want their jobs to provide career development, a sense of community, and a cause in which they can take part.[10] Each of these nonmonetary expectations is viewed as equally important to employees, and the importance of having all four expectations met is consistent, regardless of age or experience.

CAREER

Because employees are compensated based on their level of expertise, they expect each employment opportunity to grow their expertise, thus providing career advancement and greater earning power.

For most professionals, career development is somewhat random and largely dependent on the managers to whom they are assigned. There is a systemic, but mistaken, belief that an employee's career development occurs automatically year over year. That is why companies fixate on the years of experience in position descriptions.

They assume that the number of years any employee has spent in a given profession is a good representation of what that employee has actually learned over that period. However, time does not develop employees, but experiences do. For employees to grow in their career in any meaningful and prescribed way, companies must provide their employees with the right experiences, supported by the right training,

---

10 Lori Goler, Janelle Gale, Brynn Harrington, and Adam Grant, "The 3 things employees really want: Career, community, cause," Harvard Business Review, February 20, 2018, accessed October 2023, https://hbr.org/2018/02/people-want-3-things-from-work-but-most-companies-are-built-around-only-one.

at the right pace. Otherwise, "years of experience" means nothing more than "years of still breathing."

COMMUNITY

All humans have an innate need to affiliate with, and be accepted by, members of a group. They want to feel connected, respected, and recognized. All employees seek to have this need at least partially fulfilled through their job, but for professionals, this is even truer because they need to have that community experience to challenge them to deepen their knowledge and expand their expertise in their chosen field. They want to be part of a professional tribe, where they can learn from the elders and get better through competition with their peers.

CAUSE

Feeling as though their work is having a meaningful impact might have been the anomaly in the past but is the norm today. For many, doing quality work meets this need. For others, doing quality work is just not enough. They want to be a part of something that is bigger than their job, something that convinces them that they are making a difference in the lives of others.

You've no doubt heard this story before, but the message bears repeating here:

> *A man came upon a construction site where three people were working. He asked the first, "What are you doing?" and the man replied: "I am laying bricks." He asked the second, "What are you doing?" and the man replied: "I am building a wall." As he approached the third, he heard him humming a tune as he worked, and asked, "What are you doing?" The man stood, looked up at the sky, and smiled, "I am building a cathedral!"*

These expectations to feel a part of something greater directly impact an employee's longevity with a company or an industry. If you do not understand this reality and fail to incorporate it into your business design, you will be compromising your competitiveness.

Turnover

Most everyone agrees that the days of employees starting and ending their career at the same company are long gone. Because of the significant costs associated with hiring and training employees, business owners are understandably concerned with their rates of turnover.

The US Bureau of Labor Statistics (BLS) reports that service jobs currently comprise 80 percent of all US jobs.[11] Although the actual time to achieve full competency in any given service profession will vary, a conservative estimate of this time frame based on my experience is between five and seven years. According to the data reported by the BLS in 2018, the average tenure in professional and technical services is 3.9 years.[12]

The problem here is obvious.

Most employees starting out in their career will not remain with a company long enough to achieve professional competency. Since formal education only accounts for a small percentage of knowledge needed to attain professional competency, when businesses hire employees at the start of their careers, they must invest significant amounts of time or money into their professional development.

---

11   US Bureau of Labor Statistics, https://www.bls.gov/emp/tables/employment-by-major-industry-sector.htm; "News release: Employee tenure in 2018," September 20, 2018, accessed October 2023, https://stats.bls.gov/news.release/archives/tenure_09202018.pdf.

12   Ibid.

Because of these short tenures, it is very likely that another company will realize the return on their investment!

Worse, if some employers understand this, and choose not to develop their young professionals, another employer (maybe you) will over-pay for an underdeveloped employee. Depending on the percentage of younger professionals comprising the overall workforce of a given business, this phenomenon can have a significant impact on productivity and finances.

Market Fragmentation and Consolidation: Opposing Forces

Business owners have always had to compete for customers. But this competition has become even more difficult in recent years with the growing strength of two opposing forces that are impacting businesses simultaneously: market fragmentation and market consolidation. Let me explain.

Access to the internet, if nothing else, has provided us with more choices. And, when we have more choices, we tend to get more selective, seeking greater and greater specialization in our solutions. In addition, the internet has reduced our instances of human interaction, leaving us with a greater desire (a need, actually) for personal attention. These increasing desires for specialization and personal attention drive the creation of niches where none existed before, creating market fragmentation. Let's consider how the internet has impacted a product we all know—coffee.

If you were shopping for coffee in 1960, you likely had a few choices of canned, ground coffee from your local grocer that you scooped into the basket of your percolator to make your cup of morning joe.

Fast-forward sixty years.

Now, you can choose between whole bean and ground; light, dark, and medium roast; flavored and not flavored; caffeinated and decaffeinated; and chemical and water decaffeination. You can also choose between ones grown by large corporations and fair-trade co-ops. Then, with the click of a button and the instantaneous processing of your credit card, you can have your selection delivered right to your door.

To enhance your purchase experience, you can join an online community of like-minded people who are dedicated to only making fair-trade, Ethiopian coffee that is roasted at home and prepared using the French Press method.

Concurrent with this trend of market fragmentation in the form of niche explosion is market consolidation. We know that over time, markets consolidate. We have seen this happen in the banking, communications, automobile, airline, and utility industries, as a few examples. As these industries mature, small operators fail or get gobbled up by larger operators, larger operators merge, and the big keep getting bigger.

Unfortunately, for the larger businesses, more niches mean there is less pie to go around in each industry. As bigger companies try to grow in shrinking markets and smaller companies try to carve out niches, they both end up competing for the same talent pool. And as we discussed, that talent pool likes to change jobs often, has emotional needs that must be met, and is less effective and less knowledgeable than previous talent pools. Businesses that understand this dynamic have a distinct advantage over those that do not.

> **A business must be designed to anticipate and withstand chronic changes in technologies, employees, and markets.**

What's Around the Bend

I hope I have convinced you that successfully adapting to persistent changes in technology, workforce expectations, and markets without catastrophic impacts on your business requires an intentional design, one that facilitates high levels of effectiveness, efficiency, and accountability. Let me now introduce you to such a design: Sprocket.

You cannot change how someone thinks,
but you can give them a tool to use
which will lead them to think differently.

R. BUCKMINSTER FULLER

PART 2

Sprocket—The Intentional Business Design

Gets Your Business Firing on All Cylinders

To develop a new business design that resolves the deficiencies of the outdated, inherited design, I employed a well-established scientific method of making observations, developing a hypothesis to explain those observations, and testing the validity of the hypothesis. Scientists use this approach because it is a tried-and-true method. Not only does it help us successfully develop solutions to problems, but it also provides enough information so that our peers can weigh in on the soundness of the solution. My scientific approach to building a better business design, then, is as follows:

Step 1: Identify and define the fundamental components needed in a business to facilitate high levels of effectiveness, efficiency, and accountability using my direct observations of hundreds of businesses over the last three decades.

Step 2: Test the hypothesis that these fundamental components all have *equal* impacts on the effectiveness, efficiency, and accountability of the people working in the business. And if this hypothesis is

47

proved to be false, determine the relative impact of each to determine how best to optimize each.

Step 3: Test the hypothesis that these components, once optimized, would allow businesses to quickly adapt to changing conditions without sacrificing effectiveness, efficiency, or accountability.

Throughout these chapters in part 2, I will share with you the business design I developed using this approach. You will need to decide if you agree that this new design increases effectiveness, efficiency, and accountability. If you do, part 3 will show you how to apply it to your business to drive it out of yesteryear and into tomorrow.

The Fundamental Components

In science, facts are observations that have been confirmed so many times that scientists can, and for all intents and purposes do, accept as "true." Based on thirty years of observing organizations through my scientific lens, I have determined that there are five design components that are truly necessary to drive up levels of effectiveness, efficiency, and accountability among the *people* working in the business:

Purpose: This component replaces the inadequate mission/vision statement. The Purpose communicates how the business creates *value* for both customers and employees.

Strategy: This component replaces the inadequate value proposition. The Strategy identifies and leverages the *strengths* of the people operating the business and marries those strengths to the *needs and wants* of its customers.

Structure: This component replaces the inadequate organizational chart. The Structure identifies the critical functions that must be performed by the business, with a focus on optimizing *knowledge sharing* among the people who are accountable to perform these critical functions.

Processes: This component defines how things are done in the business so that actions are *consistently* both effective and efficient, results are predictable, and high levels of accountability are achieved.

Culture: This final component is nothing more than the logical outcome of incentive structures created by the combination of the business's Purpose, Strategy, Structure, and Processes. In part 3, I'll share a few simple things that you can do to supercharge your Culture.

To demonstrate why I believe that these are indeed the fundamental components of a functional business design in today's world of constant change, I am going to rely on another useful scientific tool—the equation. In science, when we want to develop a detailed description of how some aspect of the natural world behaves, we typically use math. As my advisor in graduate school drilled into my head, "If you can't write an equation to explain an observed phenomenon, you don't really understand it yet."

If I were to formulate an equation that reflected my years of observation, it would look like this.

PURPOSE + STRATEGY + STRUCTURE + PROCESSES + CULTURE = BUSINESS SUCCESS

This equation states that when all five of the truly necessary components that drive up effectiveness, efficiency, and accountability are strongly present in a business, it will be highly successful. For our purposes, we define Business Success as an efficient and effective operation, achieving high levels of accountability from the boardroom down to the mail room (if those still exist), and capable of implementing appropriate adaptive responses to changes forced on the business without disrupting the ability of the people working in the business to create value.

Wait. Isn't a successful business one that earns a substantial return on investment for the shareholders who risked their capital in the venture? Well, that's certainly one definition, but a very limiting one. A more expansive definition of business success is maximizing value—to customers, employees, and communities. And, as you'll find as you continue reading, successful businesses are the ones that are able to create value in many forms other than dollars.

What's Around the Bend

Because the equals sign (=) in our equation means that any change to the left-hand side of the equation must cause a commensurate change to the right-hand side of the equation, we can use our equation to determine the relative importance of each component to the success of a business in a qualitative sense.

In chapters 3–7, we'll explore each of our five fundamental components by defining them and investigating their individual impact on the effectiveness, efficiency, accountability, and adaptability of a business. To do that, we'll simply rewrite our equation in such a way as to indicate that a component is only weakly present and add the impact of that weakened component to the success of the business.

In chapter 8, we'll explore the collective impact of these fundamental components on a business, by focusing on the relationships among them.

Let's continue our journey.

When you're surrounded by people
who share a passionate commitment
around a common purpose,
anything is possible.

———

HOWARD SCHULTZ

CHAPTER 3

The Purpose Component

Communicates How Value Is Created

It is not what an organization *is* that's important, but it is what it *does* for others that's important. An organization's Purpose should inspire its employees, customers, partners, and community at large and serve as a call to action for them. It should function as a giant magnet, attracting only those people who are committed and loyal to the positive impact the organization is working to achieve and repelling those who are opposed or neutral.

The best way to think about a business Purpose is a *cause* to which the business is passionately committed. Missions and visions excite and motivate almost no one. Causes, on the other hand, excite and motivate everyone who believes in the cause. To have the greatest impact, the Purpose should clearly and unequivocally convey the cause to which the organization is committed, so employees can feel proud of where they choose to work, and customers can feel equally proud of where they choose to spend their money.

An organization's Purpose must communicate something more than just the products or services it provides regardless of how wonderful those products or services are or how enthusiastically the people in the organization provide them. People may love *things*, but they are only passionate about *ideas*. And, even in this age of satellite radio, everyone is still dialed into Station WII FM ("What's in it for me?"), so the Purpose must communicate to all stakeholders the value that the organization offers to *them*.

Here are three good examples of Purpose statements that succinctly convey both cause and value:

- To help our customers navigate life's twists and turns (MetLife)
- Nourishing families so they can flourish and thrive (Kellogg)
- Helping our customers build secure tomorrows (Securian Financial Group)

Don't make the mistake of thinking that a business Purpose is nothing more than a feel-good sentiment to be incorporated into marketing and branding materials. A strong Purpose that is fully embedded in an organization can positively impact customers and employees through innovation and value creation while also positively impacting the bottom line.

As an example, the *Harvard Business Review* surveyed 474 executives to explore the impact a clear sense of purpose has on business performance. The authors found that companies with a clearly articulated and understood Purpose make more money, have more engaged employees, have more loyal customers, and are better at innovation and transformational change. The gap between organizations that had a Purpose clearly articulated and understood and those that had not yet begun to develop or even think about Purpose was significant in several areas, including revenue growth, new product launches, and geographic expansion.[13] That translates into a distinct competitive advantage for Purpose-driven businesses.

It is not enough to just *have* a Purpose statement. To achieve these kinds of results, the Purpose must be thoroughly embedded throughout all functional areas of the organization. It must act as the guiding principle of the business and drive all company decisions and actions impacting both today and tomorrow. In essence, everything the business does must be considered through the lens of its Purpose.

Q: Is this action/decision we are about to take/make consistent with our stated Purpose?

Q: Will this action/decision strengthen or weaken the force of attraction we presently have with our customers and employees?

Not surprisingly, this same study showed that most of the companies surveyed had yet to embed a shared sense of Purpose throughout their organizations. Respondents cited barriers including a lack of performance targets, infrastructures that are not aligned with their Purpose, and the lack of incentives that support the Purpose. Translated into Sprocket language, they have Strategies, Structures, Processes, and Cultures that are not designed to support their Purpose. Fortunately for you, the remainder of this book will show you how to change this dynamic in your business so that you can realize the full benefits manifested by a strong Purpose.

---

13   "The business case for purpose," Harvard Business Review, April 20, 2016, accessed October 2023, https://hbr.org/sponsored/2016/04/the-business-case-for-purpose.

Impact to the Business Success Equation

What happens when a business operates with a weakly defined Purpose, leaving no clear destination toward which the organization is traveling? Confusion fills the gap. The impact of that confusion, even if all other components are strong, will diminish the organization's ability to create value by lowering levels of effectiveness, efficiency, and accountability. Therefore, we would rewrite our initial equation as follows, now using lowercase to indicate compromised components.

---

purpose + STRATEGY + STRUCTURE + PROCESSES + CULTURE = success + CONFUSION

A business Purpose conveys an organization's commitment to a cause that creates value.

What's Around the Bend

In chapter 10, I'll present a step-by-step blueprint you can follow to craft a clear Purpose statement for your organization.

But first, let's move on to the next leg of our journey where we will explore how having a weak Strategy can compromise the success of your business.

**A goal without a plan
is just a wish.**

———

ANTOINE DE SAINT-EXUPÉRY

CHAPTER 4
The Strategy Component

Leverages Your Core Competencies

The value that an organization wants to provide and to whom they want to provide it is defined in its Purpose. The details of how the organization will provide the value promised in its Purpose are defined in its business Strategy.

As with the Purpose statement, the business Strategy should be designed to provide value to customers *and* to the organization.

Before attempting to develop an effective Strategy, an organization must have clear and unambiguous answers to the following questions:

- ⚙ What do our people do best?
- ⚙ Which customers provide the most value to us?
- ⚙ What are our most valuable customers willing to give up to get our products or services?
- ⚙ How can we ensure that our products or services reflect the preferences of our most valuable customers?

These questions should convince you that if your stated business Strategy is "organic growth," you don't have a plan to achieve your stated Purpose, and therefore, you are only hoping for success, not planning for it. Let's explore these questions to learn why they are important and how thoughtfully answering them will help you transform that hope into reality.

What Do Our People Do Best?

Developing an effective Strategy starts with defining both the organizational experience and the collective individual employee education and expertise that can be leveraged to produce value for both your customers and your organization. Read that previous sentence again, because it is critically important that you understand this concept before moving forward. Developing an effective Strategy is not about looking at opportunities for making money and jumping in. It requires deciding where you want to be, based on what you do best.

I call the products or services that leverage the collective experience, education, and expertise of an organization Core Competencies.

To mitigate risk to the organization, Core Competencies must also meet a few other criteria:

- Meet the need or want within a sustainable market.
- Have a standard for performance that is met consistently.
- Have a typical completion time frame that is met consistently.
- Have a price model that consistently achieves the desired profit.
- Have a documented production process that is used consistently.

As you can see, there is a recurring theme with Core Competencies—consistency. Doing something repeatedly allows you to better your skills. We have all heard the old English proverb that "practice makes perfect." I don't know that I buy into the idea that any amount of practice will result in perfection, but I do believe that the amount of practice will determine the level of mastery. You only have to look at Michael Jordan, Simone Biles, Michael Phelps, or Serena Williams to convince yourself of that truth.

When an organization builds its Strategy around its Core Competencies (and *only* its Core Competencies), the organization's expertise in these areas will grow exponentially because of the lessons learned through repetition, giving it a significant advantage over its competitors who are less discriminating in what products or services they provide. The organization is operating strategically; its competitors are operating opportunistically.

Opportunistic businesses rank their products or services and new opportunities based almost exclusively on the ability to generate revenue. They likely (but not always) have revenue goals but rarely have detailed plans of how to achieve them. Meaning they can only hope they achieve them.

The opportunistic mindset is focused on the *urgent* (planning is a luxury that happens when "there is time"), not the *important* (planning is a priority that happens regularly).

Leaders of opportunistic businesses look at what everyone else in their industry is doing and try to do it just a little bit differently (faster, smarter) than the rest. And, if they see their competitors operating in a certain space, they jump right in with both feet. No questions asked.

Following competitors without first determining if it can offer the same products or services with consistent, positive results to ensure that maximum value is created for customers and employees alike doesn't make that organization a strategic leader in its market; it makes it an opportunistic follower.

Leaders of strategic businesses have a clear vision of their Purpose. They cultivate their Core Competencies to achieve this Purpose and make it a point to understand marketplace preferences for each core competency so that each can be tailored to those preferences.

The key to starting a fire using a magnifying glass is to hold it stationary over flammable tinder to create a spark by concentrating the sun's heat. If you keep moving the lens around, you'll never concentrate enough heat to generate that spark, let alone get a good fire burning.

Which Customers Provide the Most Value to Us?

Inherently, you know that some of your customers generate more revenue than others and this subset or another generates more profit than others. But do you know specifically which ones? To tailor your Core Competencies to customer preferences, you're going to want to zero in on only your most valuable customers; otherwise, you'll be moving that magnifying glass all over the place and squandering precious time and money.

A proven way to evaluate the value customers provide to your organization is to apply the Pareto Principle (commonly known as the 80/20 Rule). More than one hundred years ago, Vilfredo Pareto, an Italian economist, noted that 20 percent of the population in Italy owned 80 percent of the property. He hypothesized that this ratio could be found in many places in the physical world and might therefore indicate a natural law. While I don't believe there is anything magical about the numbers 20 and 80 that would indicate a natural law, I do believe that you can use the concept behind his hypothesis to maximize your Strategy by identifying your most valuable customers and quantifying their impact to your revenue and profits.

If you are not currently tracking your top revenue/profit generators, now is the time to start.

What Are Our Most Valuable Customers Willing to Give?

Because customers perceive value in terms of what they *get* compared to what they had to *give* to get it, the value from top customers can be maximized by understanding both their Give Fingerprint and their Get Fingerprint and then reflecting these back to them. Let me explain.

Businesses tend to think about what customers get from them in tangible terms, because the focus of a business is on what the organization produces. This tangible product or service meets the *functional need* of the customer. A functional need is where a customer wants something useful. For instance, they want a vacation in a warm climate to get away from a Chicago winter, or they want a new vehicle because their current one is always in the repair shop.

Many businesses (and customers!) erroneously think that purchasing decisions are only about getting functional needs met. Not true. A functional need will only *initiate* thoughts about whether or not to make a purchase. Two more important needs of the customer—their social and emotional needs—will determine whether a purchase is ultimately made and the specific selection made for that purchase.

A social need is where a customer wants access to or inclusion within a desired group that makes them feel special. For instance, a die-hard fan of a popular band might pay extra for a backstage pass to a concert so that they can snap a selfie and post a humble brag on social media implying an association with the band. Or a car enthusiast may spend untold hours and dollars refurbishing their classic car, so they'll be included in an exclusive car show where everyone will ooh and ahh over their work.

An emotional need is where a customer wants to experience a positive human emotion, such as love, joy, trust, or pride. Passionate dog owners do not buy expensive dog food to nourish their pups. They buy expensive dog food as an expression of the magnitude of their love, which makes them feel warm and fuzzy inside.

When you take the time to understand not only the functional needs but also the social and emotional needs of your most valuable customers, and match these preferences to your Core Competencies, you create lifetime customers. This unique combination of the functional, social, and emotional needs of your most valuable customers is what I call their Get Fingerprint.

There are lots of theme parks. But why do people make annual cross-country treks to Disney where they will stand in long lines wearing goofy hats to get on the same rides and see the same attractions as they did on their last seven trips? It's not the chocolate-covered ice cream in the shape of mouse ears. Disney has taken the time to define the Get Fingerprint of their most valuable customers, and they reflect those preferences in their Core Competencies.

Want to meet your favorite Disney characters (social need)? You can pay extra for a Character Meal where Disney characters meet and greet you in a restaurant setting, offering hugs, photos, autographs, or conversation. Want to feel happy (emotional need)? Why not escape reality and cold winter temperatures and visit the Happiest Place on Earth where you will only be met with smiling, courteous people who don't push, shove, or litter? It is expertly matching their Core Competencies to their most valuable customers' Get Fingerprint that makes people die-hard Disney fanatics.

But there are two sides to this coin. To get the products or services an organization provides, their most valuable customers must *give* some combination of money, time, and energy. How much they are willing to give in these arenas defines the customers' Give Fingerprint.

Your job is to make sure they get what they want without having to give more than they want.

Understanding the Get and Give Fingerprints of your most valuable customers and matching those to the Core Competencies of your business will allow you to craft a Strategy that will blow your competitors out of the water. They'll be wondering what your "secret recipe" is in a desperate attempt to replicate it. But as you now understand, they will never be able to replicate *your* Strategy because it is unique to your business, based on the core competencies of your people and the emotional needs of your most valuable customers. Competitors trying to copy your way of doing things will only make themselves less in touch with their employees and customers. So, if your present Strategy consists of monitoring your competitors and trying to emulate them, please stop.

Impact to the Business Success Equation

What happens when a business Strategy is not functioning optimally, meaning it is vague or focused only on financial outcomes? Anxiety levels rise because there is no plan to execute. The impact of that anxiety, even if all other components are strong, will diminish the organization's ability to create value by lowering levels of effectiveness, efficiency, and accountability. Therefore, we would rewrite our initial equation as follows, now using lowercase to indicate compromised components.

> **PURPOSE + strategy + STRUCTURE + PROCESSES + CULTURE = success + ANXIETY**

> **A business Strategy provides a detailed plan for internal and external value creation.**

What's Around the Bend

In chapter 11, I'll present a step-by-step blueprint you can follow to develop a focused Strategy for your organization.

But first, let's move on to the next leg of our journey where we will explore how having a weak Structure can compromise the success of your business.

Design is the intermediary
between information and understanding.

———

HANS HOFMAN

CHAPTER 5

The Structure Component

Assigns Accountabilities for Critical Functions

The impact an organization wants to have and on whom is defined in its business Purpose. How an organization chooses to provide value to its chosen target market is defined in its business Strategy.

The intent of the business Structure is to optimize organizational performance within and across functional boundaries such that value to customers *and* the organization is maximized. It is this focus on intra- (within a functional area), inter- (among functional areas), and extra- (outside the company) value creation that sets a business Structure apart from a traditional organizational chart.

To develop an effective structure, an organization must complete the following tasks:

- Define the *functional areas* needed to implement the organization's Strategy.
- Define all the high-level *responsibilities* and *accountabilities* of each functional area.

- ⚙ Determine the requisite *knowledge* that the people in each functional area need to perform their work.
- ⚙ Select the most effective way to *share* the knowledge needed in each functional area.

Functional Areas

Before we get into defining the critical functional areas needed in your operations, we must first tackle another topic that is the source of endless confusion—the distinction between governing an organization and operating it. Simply put, governing an organization consists of *steering* the organization along a chosen course via oversight, while operating an organization consists of effectively and efficiently *propelling* the organization forward along the chosen course via action. Unfortunately, the governing and operating entities of many organizations are not particularly good at staying on their side of the road. Members of governance will drift over into the operations lanes when some issue interests them. This is a dangerous practice because the main role of governance is oversight, which means monitoring, reviewing, and investigating. Who can really be objective when they are monitoring, reviewing, and investigating their own actions?

No one.

There is one area in which the governing and operating bodies must drive together in the same lane, and that is strategy development. The specific role of the governing and operating bodies in developing strategy is unique to each organization and depends on the makeup of the board and their individual and collective expertise in formulating strategy in general and, more specifically, in the industry in which the organization competes. There are three options.

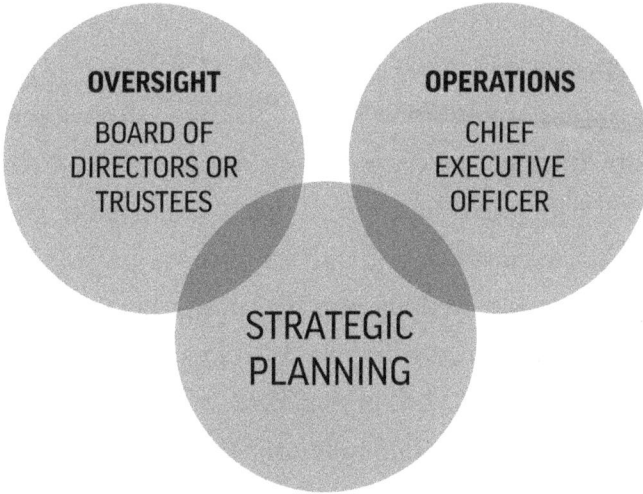

Figure 5.1

- *The board defines the strategy for the organization.* The management is responsible for developing and implementing a plan to achieve the strategy defined by the board. The board oversees its implementation and is accountable for the results.
- *The management defines the strategy for the organization and develops and implements a plan to achieve it.* The board approves the strategy, oversees its implementation, and is accountable for the results.
- *The board and management jointly define the strategy for the organization.* The management is responsible for developing and implementing a plan to achieve the strategy. The board oversees its implementation and is accountable for the results.

There is no one right way to assign responsibilities for defining the strategy. Whichever option makes the most sense for an organization in developing the strategy, the management is always responsible for implementation, and the board is always accountable for the results.

GOVERNANCE

The concept of governance is a complex beast. For instance, the International Bureau of Education within UNESCO defines governance as the "structures and processes that are designed to ensure accountability, transparency, responsiveness, rule of law, stability, equity and inclusiveness, empowerment, and broad-based participation."[14] I think the easiest way to think of it is as protecting the organization and, specifically, protecting it from *loss*—loss of reputation, loss of assets, loss of employees, loss of shareholders, loss of share price, loss of market share, loss of community confidence.

Optimizing the performance of an organization's governing body (if one exists) starts with recognizing what the owners of the organization want. In for-profit organizations, *shareholders* are the owners. They have invested their money in the organization and expect a reasonable return on their investment. In not-for-profit organizations, *stakeholders* are the owners. They are members of the public who have an interest in or who benefit from the charitable, educational, scientific, or religious purposes of the organization. They expect the organization to deliver on its promised benefits.

Since shareholders and stakeholders have no active role in the operations of the organizations in which they are monetarily or emotionally invested, they must rely on others to translate their desires into organizational performance. This is done by electing members to a governing body, most commonly a board of directors. In general, the structure of the board will be determined by the laws of the state where it operates and the bylaws of the organization. Bylaws typically determine board size, how individuals are appointed, term durations, and committee responsibilities.

---

14   UNESCO, "TVETipedia glossary," accessed October 2023, https://unevoc.unesco. org/home/TVETipedia+Glossary/lang=en/show=term/term=governance.

While directors or trustees have no responsibilities for *performing* the operational activities of the organization, they have substantial responsibilities for *overseeing* the operational activities of the organization. These responsibilities arise from their fiduciary duties—meaning they owe the corporation a duty of care, loyalty, and good faith. And, as I already mentioned, oversight is limited to monitoring, reviewing, and investigating.

While each individual director or trustee has limited powers, the board as a collection of individual directors or trustees is the ultimate authority and protector of any organization.

Since the primary work of the governing body is providing oversight, one of its main responsibilities is hiring and overseeing a competent chief executive for the organization (typically the president or CEO) who is accountable for the successful operation of the organization. It is generally the chief executive's role to hire and oversee competent executives and managers who are then accountable for the various functional areas of operations that they lead.

OPERATIONS

Because a primary role of the governing body is to provide oversight, it should not, by definition, involve itself in the day-to-day operations of an organization. Operations is the responsibility of management, which is led by the CEO and their management team.

The three critical functional areas of operations consist of the following:

- ⚙ production
- ⚙ sales
- ⚙ support

RESPONSIBILITIES AND ACCOUNTABILITIES

Responsibility refers to a person's duty to act or decide on behalf of the organization. Accountability refers to a person's ownership of the results of activities or decisions performed by themselves or others.

If a person is responsible for a task, they perform it. If a person is accountable for the same task, they assess the adequacy of the results of the completed task and take ownership of the results.

When organizations don't document who is responsible and accountable for what, they risk the following:

- Decisions take longer because no one is clear on who has the final say.
- Blame is misplaced when things go wrong.
- Areas of the organization become overworked because workloads are not balanced.
- Inactivity, because when people are not sure if they should do something, they typically do nothing.
- Employees perform tasks or make decisions for which they don't have the requisite knowledge.

Let's take a moment to define the word "accountable," since it gets tossed around a lot in the business world but is rarely well defined. As Inigo Montoya said so famously in *The Princess Bride*, "You keep using that word. I do not think it means what you think it means."

ACCOUNTABLE:

I assess the results of activities performed by me (or others), take ownership of those results, and disclose the impacts of those results in a transparent manner.

Implicit in this definition are the following assumptions:

- ✪ What tasks are to be performed (or decisions to be made) have been articulated and effectively shared.

- ✪ How the tasks are to be performed (or the latitude granted in decisions to be made) have been articulated and effectively shared.

- ✪ Who is to perform the tasks (or make the decisions) has been articulated and effectively shared.

- ✪ What a successful result looks like for any task (or decision) has been articulated and effectively shared.

If you do not ensure that your employees know what they are expected to do, how they are expected to do it, and what a successful result looks like, how can you realistically expect them to be accountable? You can't.

Manager: "Do this thing and don't screw it up."

Subordinate: "How would you like me to do it?"

Manager: "I don't know. Figure it out. That's why I pay you."

Subordinate: "Can you tell me what a successful outcome looks like?"

Manager: "If I like it, you got it right."

Subordinate: "I wasn't exactly sure what you wanted, but I gave it my best. Is this what you were looking for?"

Manager: "No. This is not at all what I wanted. How in the world did you screw this up when I told you exactly what I wanted?"

As you'll see in the next section, focusing on both the knowledge needed to perform assigned tasks and the best way to share that knowledge will help you design a Structure that results in the highest levels of accountability.

Defining Knowledge

An organization will optimize the effectiveness and efficiency of any functional area if the results it must produce are compatible with the knowledge needed to produce them. Let me explain.

There are three types of knowledge: procedure, experience, and expertise. There are also three types of products this knowledge can generate: commodity, standard, and custom. (*Note*: Wherever I use the term "products and services," this is inclusive of both internal employees and external customers.) To illustrate how knowledge types are best paired with products, I'll use the example of selling men's suits.

PROCEDURE KNOWLEDGE

Procedure knowledge comes from initially being instructed on how to perform routine tasks and then reinforcing that knowledge through the act of repetition. Because it is easy to codify the knowledge that is needed to perform these routine tasks, it is both easy and cheap to share this knowledge within the organization.

Sharing this type of knowledge can best be accomplished by using the people-to-documents model, where people create documents to impart the needed knowledge. This type of knowledge allows a functional area to have a wider span of control (number of employees to managers). Because of its low cost and high efficiency, this knowledge is best paired with the creation of commodity products or services.

Commodity products and services require the performance of a narrow range of routine tasks in which problems that arise are common and easily solved. The value of these products and services is maximized by honing the group's processes to achieve high levels of efficiency.

Let's look at how this knowledge type is paired with product type in our example of selling men's suits.

In the commodity realm of men's suits (i.e., lower-priced suits), the customer chooses the suit off the rack, and the sales associate merely needs to know how to ring up the purchase (procedural knowledge) to affect a sale.

EXPERIENCE KNOWLEDGE

As its name implies, experience knowledge comes from direct experience in performing more complex tasks. This type of knowledge is not as easily organized into procedural steps or actions because the complexity of the tasks creates more variability, making the documentation of every conceivable permutation next to impossible. Therefore, this knowledge is best shared using the people-to-people model, where more experienced employees mentor less experienced employees. This type of knowledge is more expensive than procedural knowledge to acquire, even if much of this knowledge was obtained externally (via formal education or experience at another organization), because employees with advanced knowledge command higher compensation, and mentoring requires an investment of time that cannot be passed on to the customer.

This type of knowledge is best paired with the creation of standard products and services, where employees have mastered the performance of standard types of tasks and can consistently generate quality results with little to no oversight required. When these employees do encounter nonroutine work, a more experienced employee takes over or provides specific instruction of how the work is to be performed. Therefore, this type of knowledge requires the group to have a narrower span of control (number of employees to managers).

Standard products and services require the performance of a wider range of routine tasks than do commodity types and the occasional performance of nonroutine tasks. The value of these products and services is maximized by designing the group's processes with a particular emphasis on *problem-solving*.

Using the standard model (i.e., mid-tier suits) in our example of selling men's suits, the sales associates are more experienced in choosing the right suit for each customer, accessorizing the suit, and communicating the value to purchasing a complete outfit. The ability to upsell through experience-based knowledge results in higher value to the customer and the business.

EXPERTISE KNOWLEDGE

Expertise knowledge begins from a primarily experience-based place until employees have honed that experience to the point where they can successfully use their intuition to predict outcomes for standard work and develop new outcome models for situations they have not previously encountered.

This type of knowledge is prohibitively costly to codify or communicate. It cannot be leveraged within the group, and therefore, the group must rely on "rock star" employees who have acquired remarkable knowledge that is used to create custom products and services. With this type of knowledge, there is essentially no span of control as employees are wholly responsible for their own work with little to no oversight required.

Custom products and services require the performance of a wide range of nonroutine tasks. The value of these products and services can only be maximized through the acquisition and retention of those rock stars.

Selling men's suits in the custom model (i.e., luxury brands) requires a highly talented and experienced tailor with expertise knowledge who creates a unique suit with a custom fit that is made from a fabric chosen to specifically reflect the personality of the customer.

Warning: Many businesses fall into the trap of thinking that what they do is "custom" even when it is not. I think this happens for two reasons. One, it just feels better to think you are "one-of-a-kind." But this only serves to elevate your status in your own mind. Two, it lets you off the hook of doing the hard but important work of determining how things should be done, documenting those decisions, and educating your employees on how to implement. Don't hamstring your business by making that mistake.

Special Considerations for Knowledge

LIFE CYCLE

For production teams, the knowledge possessed and needed will be dictated by the current life cycle stage of the organization. This cycle can most simply be divided into three distinct stages where each presents them with different opportunities and challenges:

- *New:* In this life cycle stage, everything is new. Production teams should focus on acquiring new knowledge to better define and deliver their products or services. Where businesses are new to their markets, but their products or services are not, knowledge-based documents should be relied on to help compete with at-scale players.

- *Developing:* In this life cycle stage, knowledge required is more defined, stable, and therefore easier to codify. Production teams should focus on optimizing the complementarity between value creation and knowledge leverage. The goal should be an intensive use of existing knowledge to increase value for the organization.

○ *Mature:* In this life cycle phase, products or services are standardized. Production teams should focus on improving the codifiability and integration of knowledge for existing products and services while adding new ones to ensure growth and differentiation.

WORK FROM HOME

The institutional knowledge that exists in any of the three functional areas of operations (Production, Sales, and Support) is the *combined* education, expertise, and experience of its employees. This institutional knowledge can span years or decades and thus will shape the perspectives of and processes used within the functional area. This institutional knowledge can be broken down into two groups:

○ *Explicit* or *tangible knowledge*, including documents, records, and reports that can be stored and easily shared with others.

○ *Implicit* or *intangible knowledge*, including personal experiences, skills, and intuition that are more difficult to share with others and so are best shared through training and mentoring.

Although the distinction between these two types of knowledge has always been important, it has become even more important in the new dynamic of work-from-home (WFH) or hybrid (part in-office, part at-home) work arrangements. The COVID-19 pandemic has shown us that transferring implicit or intangible knowledge throughout an organization using virtual meetings can be very difficult indeed.

We've all experienced these three types of knowledge when purchasing a product or service. Here are two of my varied experiences for the same product. I was once looking to buy an electronic keyboard as a gift. I was in a discount electronics store and was reading the descriptions of a few options on the shelf when a sales associate approached me and asked if they could help. I said I was looking for an electronic keyboard, but since I don't play one myself, I was not sure what the differences were between the products in front of me based on their descriptions. The sales associate then proceeded to read each information card to me. They offered no context for any of the descriptive language. Since I have known how to read since I was five, I ended up feeling more frustrated and annoyed by the addition of this so-called help than if I had just been left to my own devices.

Compare that with the local music shop in our town that I recently visited. This is not a store where people go to buy musical instruments; it is a place where musicians gather to discuss their craft and buy the perfect instrument or accessory to further develop that craft.

There is a special soundproof and climate-controlled room for the wood guitars, comfy chairs, and amplifiers where patrons can try out a variety of electric guitars, a stage in another room with a full drum set (and bongos!). Everything is designed to allow customers to play their music on the store's merchandise before selecting and making a purchase.

The employees don't ask if you need help, because it is *understood* that you will ask questions *if* you have any. And they will respond to your question with clarifying questions of their own to ensure they understand exactly what type of music you are playing so that they can recommend a few good options that are tailored to your needs.

Sharing Knowledge

Once you have the knowledge type and product type better matched in a functional area, performance can be enhanced by selecting the appropriate span of control (the number of employees to managers), which will depend not only on the type of knowledge required by the area's employees but also on how that knowledge is best shared.

As an example, if production is attempting to provide a high-value product or service without its employees having the requisite knowledge, employees will frequently encounter problems they cannot resolve and will have to refer these unresolved problems to more knowledgeable employees, typically managers.

If there is a wide span of control (high number of employees to managers), performance suffers because the production employees are incapable of being *effective* (because they keep running into problems they can't solve), and the production managers are incapable of being *efficient* (because they are spending an excessive amount of time solving their subordinates' problems).

In this scenario, resolving this value-to-knowledge gap will require a significant investment in acquiring and integrating the requisite knowledge for the production team to perform successfully under the existing span of control. We can go back to our use of an equation to see that we can only increase value by making a commensurate increase in knowledge.

$$\boxed{\textbf{KNOWLEDGE = VALUE}}$$

If an organization is not capable of increasing knowledge, or simply can't afford it, the value position would need to be lowered to avoid sacrificing performance by either reducing the span of control or deciding to produce a product that better fits the team's collective knowledge and the existing span of control.

Many firms invest in information and communication technologies to assist with the sharing of institutional knowledge. These technologies are highly effective in increasing the efficiencies associated with procedural knowledge because it is highly codifiable. Some additional efficiencies can be obtained when used with experience-based knowledge if the technologies are focused on problem-solving and mentoring. However, it is important to understand that these technologies are rarely effective in creating additional efficiencies when applied to expertise knowledge, because while it is easy to share information that can be codified, it is not easy to share information that is intuitive. That may all soon change with the development of and access to artificial intelligence, but only time will tell.

Impact on the Business Success Equation

A business Structure must distinguish between governance and operations. Within operations, the primary responsibilities and accountabilities of each functional area must be defined. Within each functional area, the knowledge required to perform at a high level must be identified, and the most effective means of sharing that knowledge must be implemented.

What happens when a business Structure is not functioning optimally, meaning it does not focus on the critical functions of the business and the knowledge needed to perform those functions? Redundancies and gaps in operations are created. The impact of those redundancies and gaps, even if all other components are strong, will diminish the organization's ability to create value by lowering levels of effectiveness, efficiency, and accountability. Therefore, we would rewrite our initial equation as follows, now using lowercase to indicate compromised components.

PURPOSE + STRATEGY + structure + PROCESSES +
CULTURE = success + REDUNDANCIES/GAPS

A business Structure is designed to optimize performance within and across functional boundaries to maximize internal and external value.

What's Around the Bend

In chapter 12, I'll present a step-by-step blueprint you can follow to design a solid Structure for your organization.

But first, let's move on to the next leg of our journey where we will explore how having weak Processes can compromise the success of your business.

**Everything should be
made as simple as possible,
but not simpler.**

———

ALBERT EINSTEIN

CHAPTER 6
The Processes Component

Defines Your Ideal Ways to Get Work Done

The impact an organization wants to have, and on whom, is defined in its Purpose. How an organization chooses to provide value to its chosen target market is defined in its business Strategy. How resources are allocated within an organization to maximize value creation defines its business Structure.

The intent of business Processes is to ensure that the organization is protected from risk and operates with high levels of integrity, effectiveness, efficiency, and accountability. Organizational Processes provide a road map for conducting day-to-day operations by guiding decision-making, streamlining internal workflows, and maximizing the quality of outcomes produced.

When I use the term "Processes" in this book, I am using one umbrella term to represent four different types of documents, each with its own specific role in directing, administering, and managing an organization: Rules, Policies, Processes, and Procedures. It's important that you understand what each type of document can achieve for your organization and how to use each for maximum effect.

To explain the function of each document, let's assume that you are a truck driver making a delivery to a new destination. As the driver, you need to have a valid commercial driver's license and insurance. You understand that each state that you drive through has its own laws to keep the roads safer for all that use them and that if you don't comply and get caught, you will face some type of punishment (e.g., a ticket, fine, or jail time). You also know that if you are found responsible for an accident, your company will fire you because of its zero-tolerance safety stance. These state laws along with your company's stance on safety represent the *rules*.

You generally avoid toll roads because of the high costs but make it a practice to evaluate whether using them on a given trip can save you more in fuel costs because of a shorter drive time. This decision model represents the *policy*.

Using your vehicle GPS system, you select the best route to get to your destination based on travel time and total costs. The route you take represents the *process*.

Enabling the turn-by-turn directions of your GPS system, you would be told exactly where to make turns, change lanes, or exit the highway. These step-by-step instructions represent the *procedure*.

These four elements, when used in combination, help you travel safely and efficiently to your destination by ensuring that you don't get a ticket, get lost, or overspend on gas and tolls.

In my experience, there is a general lack of understanding in organizations of the differences between these documents. Rules get conflated with policies, policies get conflated with processes, and processes get conflated with procedures. All of these conflations result in a dizzying array of documents that creates more confusion within the organization, not less.

If you set a table for a dinner party where each place setting is provided with a fork, knife, and spoon, most of your guests will select the most appropriate utensil to eat the soup, salad, and steak you serve. However, if everyone just gets a spork (spoon-fork combo), eating that soup, salad, and steak is going to get messy.

Without proper documentation and understanding of their intention, employees tend to act based on what they think they remember about the respective rules, policies, processes, and procedures an organization has. Such an approach is fraught with error and waste and results in low levels of accountability across the organization, compromising both employee confidence and morale.

When guidance documents are created that conflate the intentions of these four different types of documents, they tend to be quite lengthy. While they may be read, it's a coin toss as to whether they are well understood, sufficiently remembered, or even used.

Rules

Every organization is subject to laws and regulations imposed by local, state, and federal governments. In general, these laws and regulations are designed to create and keep order, protect property, provide a sense of fair play, and keep people safe.

By their nature, laws and regulations are intended to hold *everyone* to the same standard, and consequences for noncompliance are predetermined and do not generally vary based on conditions or circumstances. To avoid fines, lawsuits, and/or diminished reputation, all organizations must acknowledge and clearly communicate their position on compliance with the laws and regulations imposed on it to ensure that all its employees strictly comply with them.

In addition, organizations typically have a set of internal rules that, if violated, can have significant adverse or even catastrophic consequences. These internal rules prescribe minimum acceptable behavior that is applicable to *everyone* in the organization and the consequences that will result if violated. These internal rules demand full compliance with no allowance for personal discretion. They are enforced stringently because the risk to the organization for noncompliance is simply too great.

Policies

Policies are best reserved for providing *guidance* on decision-making under various circumstances to ensure uniformity in the ultimate decisions being made.

It confuses employees when the label "policy" is used for a document that conveys both rules and guidance. They can end up thinking that all instructions in the document should be considered as merely guidance, so they are free to make all decisions based on their own judgment and at their own discretion. Conversely, they can end up thinking that all instruction in the document should be considered hard-and-fast rules with no flexibility, leading them to get approval from their supervisors on every decision to avoid possibly getting into hot water. It is much better to distinguish between rules and guidance documents if you want employees to make the right decisions and assume accountability for those decisions.

Policies should be developed and communicated at the departmental level to provide *predetermined decisions* to common issues the department encounters regularly. Properly written, they should guide the decision-making process by including typical responses and the acceptable limits of judgment and discretion for each position within the department authorized to participate in that decision-making process.

Wherever possible, policies should facilitate the ability of lower-level positions within the department to make decisions appropriate for their position without the need to consult higher-level positions before deciding or get approval after deciding. In essence, they should serve as standing decision-making trees for recurring issues.

Processes

Although policies guide *decision-making* at the departmental level and the latitude that individual roles have in making these decisions, processes guide *actions* taken by employees at the departmental level.

A process defines the high-level view of tasks that need to be performed to achieve an objective, the order in which they are best performed, who performs them, and who is accountable for their successful completion. The distinction between policies and processes is that the latter have a start and end with distinct steps in between.

A common refrain within organizations is "we don't have a process for that," even when the organization has performed actions to achieve the required outcome countless times. Though unaware, these organizations do, in fact, have a process in place, it is just not documented, and since it is not documented, there is a high probability that the process is not followed consistently, may not be effective, and almost certainly is not efficient.

More dangerously, the process may only be known by one individual, and when they leave the organization, that process goes right out the door with them.

A process is only as good as a user's ability to understand it. If it is difficult to understand and hard to use, it just won't work as intended. Ineffective processes have these things in common:

- They are not documented well (if at all).
- They are difficult to understand.
- They are inconsistent (and sometimes even incorrect).

Most organizations record their processes in content-dense, written documents that are anything but simple to use. Lengthy process documents are fine as reference materials, but if that is all you offer your employees, you run the risk that the documents won't be read, making your painstakingly crafted documents all but useless.

Procedures

A process tells the team *what* needs to be done, but it does not tell them *how* to do it.

A procedure is needed to define the detailed steps required to perform the tasks identified in the process. This is a critical element that is so often lacking because "everyone knows how to do it."

Processes look at the big picture, while procedures detail individual tasks associated with those processes.

Procedure documents are necessary to ensure that tasks are performed in a consistent way to meet the organization's need to limit risk and ensure quality. In essence, they force the organization to decide how something *should be done* to ensure that efforts expended to obtain desired results are appropriate. They also encourage continuous improvement by allowing changing conditions to be easily accommodated.

Not every activity requires a procedure document. For instance, if a required task is to complete a form and there are explicit and clear instructions of how to do so printed on the form, a procedure document would only be redundant.

However, if it is not completely obvious how any task identified in a process should be performed, a procedure document should be developed. If you are whipping up some cookies for yourself, you may not need a recipe. However, if you own a bakery and sell cookies for a living, you must have a recipe your employees can follow to ensure that they produce a consistent product, and you can earn a consistent profit.

Accessibility and Utilization

As you now understand, having an effective set of rules, policies, processes, and procedures is vital if you want critical business functions to be successfully fulfilled without any undue risk to the organization or its employees.

But, even the most complementary set of documents will do an organization no good unless its employees have ready access to them, understand them, and use them correctly and consistently.

Many organizations prepare these types of documents, provide them to their employees to read, require them to attest to having read and understood them, and assume that their job is done. The harsh reality is that preparing these documents, and getting employees to read and understand them, is only the *first* step. Making them an integral part of operations is the *most important* step.

Impact on the Business Success Equation

What happens when business Processes are not functioning optimally, meaning the business does not have and/or use the proper documentation? Frustration thrives. The impact of that pervasive frustration, even if all other components are strong, will diminish the organization's ability to create value by lowering levels of effectiveness, efficiency, and accountability. Therefore, we would rewrite our initial equation as follows, now using lowercase to indicate compromised components.

> **PURPOSE + STRATEGY + STRUCTURE + processes + CULTURE = success + FRUSTRATION**

Organizational Processes provide a road map for conducting day-to-day operations by guiding decision-making, streamlining workflows, and maximizing the quality of outcomes produced.

What's Around the Bend

In chapter 13, I'll present a step-by-step blueprint you can follow to design effective and efficient Processes for your organization.

But first, let's move on to the next leg of our journey where we will explore how having a weak Culture can compromise the success of your business.

Determine what behaviors
you value as a company
and have everyone live true to them.
These behaviors and beliefs should be
so essential to your core that you
don't even think of it as culture.

BRITTANY FORSYTH

CHAPTER 7

The Culture Component

Creates Incentive Structures That Work

In 1944, Harold Samuel, a real estate tycoon in the United Kingdom, coined the expression: "There are three things that matter in property: location, location, location." What he was conveying was that even if homes are the same size, built in the same year, and share many of the same or even identical features, they may vary greatly in value depending on where they are located. And, even though location is considered to be the number one rule in real estate, it is often the most overlooked rule as well.

Borrowing heavily from Lord Samuel, we can say that there are three things that matter in business culture: design, design, design. Even companies of the same size and market penetration that produce similar products can have very different cultures depending on their business design. Just as you can buy the right home in the wrong location, you can doom a good company with a lousy culture by using the wrong business design. Don't be the leader who overlooks the importance of business design.

Culture is commonly defined as the combined beliefs, behaviors, values, and attitudes of the people in an organization. Some refer to it as the organization's "personality" or "way of life." The presumption here is that each person in the organization brings to it their individual—preordained or preformulated—sensibilities. When all of these individual sensibilities are brought together under the same roof, the composite result creates the culture of the organization.

So, fixing a bad culture should be no more complicated than changing the sensibilities of the troublemakers (the ones who are not engaged, feel entitled, or create a toxic environment). And if their sensibilities can't be changed, get rid of them. Right? Wrong.

Despite what you may read or hear to the contrary, you cannot improve the culture of an organization by trying to change (manipulate, really) the sensibilities of the people within it, because culture is not the aggregate of the personal points of view of its people. Culture is, and always has been, the aggregate of how its people individually respond to their organization's design. Let me explain.

Your Purpose, Strategy, Structure, and Processes (or the lack thereof) are individually and collectively creating incentives in your organization whether you are aware of them or not. The people in your organization are acting and making decisions every day in accordance with *their* understanding of how these incentives can be used to benefit *them*. Taken together, all these unique understandings of your intended or unintended incentives define the Culture of your business. The people in an organization do not manifest its Culture independently of its Purpose, Strategy, Structure, and Processes but rather in *direct response to it*. If your business was not intentionally designed with a full understanding of how these four fundamental components impact the Culture of your organization, tasking your

HR department to "fix" your Culture is analogous to painting the house in an effort to "fix" its undesirable location. It won't work.

To develop and maintain a harmonious Culture, meaning all the arrows are pointed in the same direction, an organization must thoughtfully design its business to create the right incentive structures. If you already have a harmonious culture and want to turn it into a fantastically harmonious one, you'll want to consider implementing some of the suggestions found in chapter 14.

What does a fantastically harmonious culture look like, you ask? It is one where every employee could honestly say, "I know what this organization is trying to accomplish. I know exactly how my work fits into the big picture here. I have the guidance I need to do my work at a high level without the need to guess or constantly ask questions of my supervisor. I know which behaviors are valued and rewarded, and I feel aligned with those values."

Let's explore the types of incentives commonly used in organizations and how these may be working for or against you to create that harmonious culture.

Incentives

An incentive is anything that motivates a person to do something. There are two types of incentives that affect human action:

- *Intrinsic incentives* are internal motivators. They are innate, inherent, and essential to the individual. A person wants to do something, without any fear of punishment or promise of a reward, because they are motivated by a sense of personal fulfillment or satisfaction.

- *Extrinsic incentives* are external motivators. They are not essential to the individual. They involve the promise of a reward for accomplishing a task or the threat of a punishment for failure to do so. All financial incentives and rules are strictly of the extrinsic type.

The combined set of intrinsic and extrinsic incentives an organization uses to influence the choices made by its people is known as the organization's *incentive structure*. With a poorly designed incentive structure, or one created by default, employees are frequently forced to choose between what is in *their* best interests and what is in the *organization's* best interests.

The goal of an effective incentive structure is to create congruency between the best interests of the employee and the organization so that the employee does not have to choose between serving the interests of one at the sacrifice of the other. It's about eliminating win-lose dynamics and creating win-win dynamics for your employees.

When employees understand and believe that what is in the best interest of the organization is also in their own personal best interest, the organization can significantly increase accountability, empowerment, morale, and retention. In other words, they create a harmonious culture.

INTRINSIC INCENTIVES

If intrinsic incentives are innate, meaning people are born with them, how can a business possibly ensure that everyone in its diverse workforce be intrinsically motivated while fulfilling their day-to-day responsibilities? Like many things in the scientific world, the answer is both simple and elegant. You cannot influence the intrinsic motivators of your employees, but you can purposefully attract people to your organization whose natural inclinations are to behave in ways that are aligned with how you would like them to behave. This starts with having a strong Purpose that acts like a magnet to attract employees who are inspired by and committed to your Purpose. You then supercharge your Purpose with Core Values.

The Core Values of an organization reflect the intentional experience it wants all stakeholders (shareholders, employees, customers, suppliers, and community members) to have in every interaction. As with Purpose, Core Values are not just another trendy marketing ploy. Nor are they lofty aspirations like what you see printed on posters in HR Director offices. Core Values are a commitment to how your business is run every single day. They are ingrained and sacrosanct. They are integrated into every employee-related process, including performance appraisals, promotions, and bonuses. When integrated successfully, employees *experience* the Core Values of their organization as the standards for all decisions and actions at the organizational, departmental, and individual levels. They do not just see them published on business cards and websites; they live and breathe them.

There are three main categories of values used in the business environment, but only one will result in employees behaving in a desired manner toward all other employees, customers, and visitors and therefore are suitable to serve as Core Values:

- ✪ *Standard values* reflect minimum social or industry standards. Examples of this type of value are honesty, competency, responsibility, and respect. Because these values are *expected*, they add nothing to the intrinsic motivation of employees.

- ✪ *Personality values* reflect the common interests of the organization's employees. Examples of this type of value are unconventional, fun, passionate, and creative. These values *can* increase the intrinsic motivation of employees, but they do have a few downsides.

   First, they can limit the diversity of the workforce. For example, if an organization's values convey everyone is young and hip, it excludes the middle-aged woman with decades of relevant experience. Likewise, if its values convey everyone is fun and boisterous, it may exclude the highly creative introvert who suffers from social anxiety.

This popular tribal mentality should be approached cautiously, if at all. The desire to make everyone feel included creates a mandate for sameness and can have the unintended consequence of making some employees feel excluded because of their differences.

Also, these personality values are focused on employees, and they may not align well with the organization's stakeholders. For instance, if the company leaders encourage a vibe that the organization wants to be seen as unconventional or disruptive, that may attract and energize a younger workforce but may repel and worry shareholders and lenders.

○ *Leadership/Founder values* reflect the values of the organization's current leadership team (or original founders) and therefore are the only values that can serve as true Core Values. Transformative decisions will be made by your leadership team, and if these decisions are to be truly guided by your Core Values, they must be values embraced and embodied by that team. They cannot be feel-good values that are not the true standard of the organization, or they will ring hollow and will never be effectively infused throughout the organization.

Core Values should not be defined by soliciting input from your employees and going with the opinion of the majority. The truth is you may currently have employees with the wrong set of values for your organization—so you don't want them helping to define your

Core Values. These values are too important to the success of your organization to leave them up to some sort of popularity contest.

With Core Values ingrained in your operation, your employees will not need to subconsciously ask, "Is this task I am performing or decision I am making consistent with our Core Values?" because they naturally act consistently with your Core Values. To enhance the intrinsic motivation of employees, attain behaviors toward all stakeholders your organization desires, and fulfill your Purpose, only Core Values based on Leadership/Founder values will do.

EXTRINSIC INCENTIVES

Extrinsic incentives are based on a reward system of "do this and you'll get that." It is a reward system used so extensively by parents, teachers, coaches, and supervisors that it is woven into the fabric of American life. A reward system that is based on a pervasive, but rarely examined, belief that humans will do a better job if they have been promised some sort of *reward*, be that extra TV time, good grades, praise, attention, money, or promotion. There is no argument that this reward system is ubiquitous, but does that mean it's effective?

According to Alfie Kohn of the *Harvard Business Review*, at least two dozen studies have conclusively shown that people who expect a reward for completing a task or for doing that task successfully simply do not perform as well as those who expect no reward at all. The researchers found that for children and adults—males and females—the more cognitive sophistication and open-ended thinking were required, the worse research subjects performed when working for a reward.[15]

---

15   Alfie Kohn, "Why incentive plans cannot work," Harvard Business Review, September-October 1993, accessed October 2023, https://hbr.org/1993/09/why-incentive-plans-cannot-work.

In addition, if rewards are used to stimulate behaviors that an individual *already* finds motivating, intrinsic motivation for that behavior may decrease over time. This can lead to extinguishing intrinsic motivation and creating a dependence on extrinsic rewards for continued performance. And, like any good dependence, the need for the "fix" only grows. According to Tomas Chamorro-Premuzic of the *Harvard Business Review*, "For every standard deviation increase in reward, intrinsic motivation for interesting tasks decreases by about 25 percent. When rewards are tangible and foreseeable (if subjects know in advance how much extra money they will receive) intrinsic motivation decreases by 36 percent."[16]

Rewards have a negative effect on intrinsic motivation because anything seen as a prerequisite for something else is seen as less desirable. Consider general education requirements in college curriculums. The prerequisite courses are the boring courses you must take so that you will be granted access to the higher-level courses in your major that are more interesting to you and more relevant for your chosen career.

When my oldest son got his first report card with letter grades in elementary school, he made a point of telling me how much money other parents were paying their children for every "A" they received. He assumed he would also be handsomely rewarded for his impressive report card. Much to his dismay, this did not happen.

I explained to him that he had to decide the quality of life he wanted to have and that, in my opinion, becoming educated was the most important thing a person could do to achieve a good quality of life. He would have to decide how much he wanted to invest in

---

16   Tomas Chamorro-Premuzic, "Does money really affect motivation? A review of the research," Harvard Business Review, April 10, 2013, accessed October 2023, https://hbr.org/2013/04/does-money-really-affect-motiv.

his own future. He kept getting good grades, but only because it was important to him, not because he was working for a big pay day.

Rewards and punishment are two sides of the same coin. Rewards are no less manipulative than punishments. Not receiving a reward that was expected is indistinguishable in the human mind from being punished.

Several years ago, I was contacted by a leader at a local nonprofit who was calling to express confusion as to why they did not receive one of our Charitable Giving Grants although they had received the past two years. I explained (again) that all our applications are reviewed by our employees, and *they* choose the recipients based on what is at the top of mind for *them*.

My explanation was met with, "But we were counting on that and now our budget is blown. This is a big problem. Why did you give our money to another nonprofit without telling us?" This organization had an expectation of a reward (an unrealistic expectation given how our program is designed) and not receiving it felt like a punishment.

Although rewards come in many forms, it is monetary rewards that businesses use most extensively. This is due to a fundamental assumption in the field of economics that people will almost always act in a way that will improve their economic standing. However, there is no scientific basis for the assumption that paying people more will encourage them to do *better* work. People are concerned about their salaries, of course, but this does not mean that money is necessarily motivating them to do *good* work. According to Frederick Herzberg, distinguished professor of management at the University of Utah's Graduate School of Management, "It is plausible to assume that if someone's take-home pay was cut in half, his or her morale would suffer enough to undermine performance. But it doesn't necessarily follow that doubling that person's pay would result in better work."[17]

The improper use of monetary rewards to influence employee behavior can result in any (or all) of the following unintended consequences:

- Reduced cooperation within teams as individuals compete for a reward.
- Employees hide problems rather than asking for help to not risk losing a reward.
- The organization ignores what employees really need to do a good job, using the reward as a poor substitute.
- Employees put a priority on quantity over quality, compromising the customer experience.
- A heightened desire for simplicity and predictability, resulting in less prudent risk-taking.
- More focus on the "that" and not the "this" in the "do this and you'll get that" bribe.

Unfortunately, when a monetary rewards program is not getting desired results, organizations mistakenly believe it is due to some inadequacy of the program and not the psychological assumptions that are the basis of the program. This results in futile attempts to fine-tune the calculations and/or delivery of the rewards program.

This has been the failed approach in the business world since the 1950s when the behaviorist theory derived from experiments with laboratory animals first suggested that programs such as piecework for factory workers, stock options for executives, special privileges for the employee of the month, and commissions for salespeople might be effective motivators in the workplace.

---

17   Alfie Kohn, "Why incentive plans cannot work."

However, because monetary rewards are nothing more than bribes, no amount of program fine-tuning will ever result in effectively changing the long-term employee behavior. Rewards do not alter attitudes that underlie human behaviors. They do not create an enduring commitment to any action or value associated with that action. They merely, and temporarily, change what is done. That change is limited to *quantitative*, not *qualitative*, metrics. They lead to producing *more*, not to producing *better*.

This is not to say that monetary reward programs are bad. On the contrary, when done correctly, they are good, because they communicate that the organization values its employees, which helps attract and retain them. They show employees that their efforts are integral to the financial success of the organization and reward their contribution to that financial success.

As discussed previously, extrinsic incentives are fraught with problems, including unanticipated and undesirable behavioral responses when they are focused on *outputs*. To ensure effective responses by employees to a financial incentive, the incentive must reward the conduct or behaviors that employees can *control*. In most cases, employees have significantly more control over *inputs* than over *outputs*.

To be an effective incentive, monetary reward programs must affect employee *behavior* (inputs) on the job, day in and day out. This does not happen when the rewards are paid out once a year, at the management's discretion. When implemented like this, employees rarely know what they must do to get the reward other than doing a "good job." And, after this subjective assessment by the employee, if a reward is not given, the employee will feel punished and disappointed. Quite the opposite outcome from the intention of the program.

Creating a monetary rewards program to serve as an effective extrinsic incentive to drive the right behaviors by employees *can* be done. But it is not for the faint of heart, requiring a significant commitment of time and effort on the part of the organization and its department supervisors.

Businesses often see an undesirable culture as being the result of the people in the organization. These businesses will focus on the people of the organization to fix a "broken" culture rather than on the business design and incentive structures resulting from that design. This is tantamount to entering the highway from the exit ramp. I did this once as a new driver many moons ago when visiting England. I don't recommend it.

IMPACT ON THE BUSINESS SUCCESS EQUATION

What happens if a business has a clear Purpose, a focused Strategy, and a solid Structure supported by effective and efficient Processes, but these elements are not working together in a holistic and integrated manner with the organization's Core Values to define the proper incentive structures? Productivity and profitability will decline, resulting in *lackluster results* associated with value creation because of a misalignment between the goals of the employees and the goals of the organization. Therefore, we would rewrite our initial equation as follows, now using lowercase to indicate compromised components.

**PURPOSE + STRATEGY + STRUCTURE + PROCESSES +
culture = success + LACKLUSTER RESULTS**

> **A business Culture is nothing more than the aggregate of how employees respond to the incentive structures created by the design of the organization.**

What's Around the Bend

In chapter 14, I'll present a step-by-step blueprint you can follow to further enhance the Culture in your organization even after you have optimized all other components in your business design.

But before I share with you how to optimize the five components of the Sprocket business design, there is another scientific concept that I would like to explain that will set the stage for understanding how these elements work together in your organization.

A system is a set of related components that work together in a particular environment to perform whatever functions are required to achieve the system's objective.

DONELLA MEADOWS

CHAPTER 8

Applying Systems Theory to This Design

Eliminates Silos

In the introduction to part 2, we stated that to improve on the design that most businesses use (as explained in part 1), we would need to identify and define the true fundamental components that help an organization operate effectively and efficiently by investigating what happens when each component is missing.

The qualitative assessment we undertook in chapters 3 through 7 helped us to understand the *relative importance* of each component to business success by exploring what happens to operations when each component was not functioning optimally.

We also stated that we would need to test the hypothesis that these fundamental components all have *equal* impacts on the effectiveness and efficiency of the business, and if this hypothesis was proved to be false, determine the relative impact of each.

If we want to understand the *proportional importance* of each component to business success, we can no longer consider a business as a set of independent components operating in segregated silos but must consider it as a *system of interrelated components*, where business success is dependent not only on the effectiveness and efficiency of each component but also on the *relationships* among these components.

Relationships among components in a system are not neutral. They are either positive and constructive, where they create synergies, or negative and destructive, where they create interferences.

Systems Theory

Systems theory is a conceptual framework based on the principle that the component parts of a system can best be understood in the context of the relationships with one another and with other systems rather than in isolation. When applied to business, this theory asserts that any organization is a single, unified system of interrelated parts, where each part is dependent on the others and cannot function optimally without them.

Let me give you an analogy of systems theory from your everyday life. Most of us use a car to get ourselves around. Even if you don't drive, chances are high that you have ridden in one at some point. Unless you are an automotive mechanic or a motorhead, you probably don't think much about what must happen to make the car move. You just start the ignition, step on the gas, and off you go.

The movement of a car is controlled by its power train, which consists of the engine, transmission, drive shaft, differential, axles, and wheels. These parts work together to move the car forward in a specific and controlled manner. They are a system. In this system, the engine transforms fuel into energy, which is then sequentially transferred to the drive shaft, differential, axles, and wheels to make the car move.

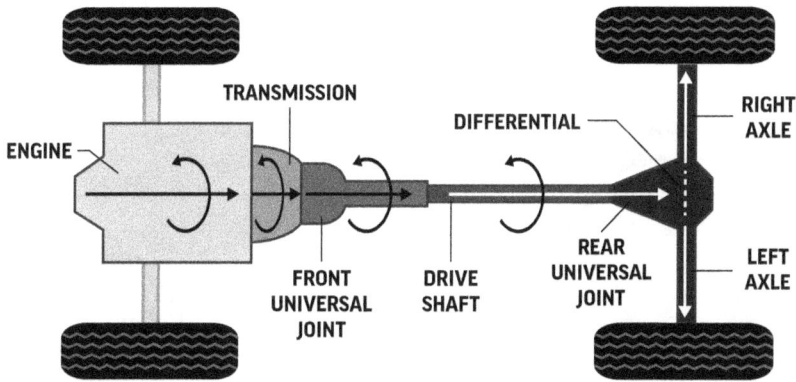

Figure 8.1

We can use this system as an analogy for a business design since it too is intended to move something forward in a specific and controlled manner—in this case, your business. Applying this analogy, we can consider our Purpose as the engine, our Strategy as the transmission, our Structure as the drive shaft, our Processes as the differential and axles, and our Culture as the wheels. In essence, our Purpose provides the energy needed to power our Strategy, Structure, and Processes, which all work together to create a Culture that propels our business forward. Like the powertrain of a car, all the components of the business design must work together to ensure that the business travels in the right direction and at the right speed, avoiding all hazards along the way that could push the business into a ditch or oncoming traffic.

If we wanted to create a simpler graphic to represent our business as a system, we could use a series of interlocking sprockets. Maintaining our analogy between a business design and a car powertrain, we would choose the placement of each sprocket based on energy transfer to and from that particular component, and we would choose the size of each sprocket based on the importance of this energy transfer (its proportional importance) within the business. The result would be the graphic presented next.

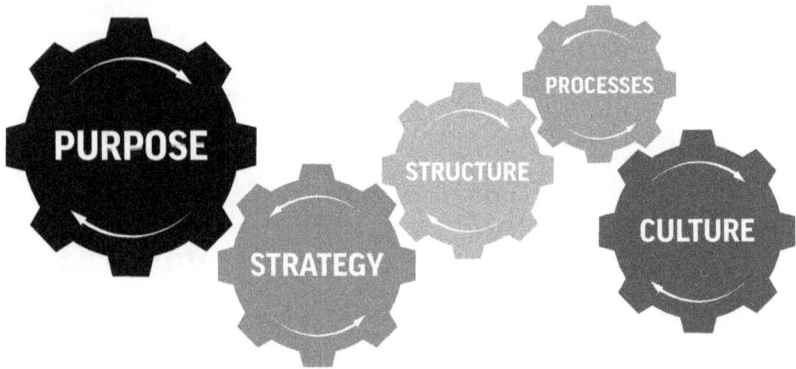

Figure 8.2

RELATIONSHIPS IN THE SYSTEM

We've already considered the impact on business success when any individual component is not functioning optimally. But what happens to the effectiveness and efficiency of our business if any of the sprockets are not in the right position or are not the right size?

If the business Purpose is not given the primary position within the business or is undersized, you may see a Strategy that is opportunistic, resulting in a Structure that puts an emphasis on power and authority rather than function. Processes, if documented at all, are only developed for the worker bees, resulting in a Culture where accountability is very low throughout the organization.

If the business Strategy component is undersized, the business will constantly chase what its competitors are chasing. The business will frequently undergo a restructuring, as it reinvents itself to accommodate the latest products or services it is offering. But, because these new products or services were not chosen based on their alignment with the business Purpose (meaning there was an inadequate focus on internal and external value creation), the company restructures again when these new products or services don't perform as hoped.

If the Structure component is wrongly given the primary position within the system, under the mistaken notion that putting the "right people" in the "right place" is all that is needed for the system to operate efficiently, the entire flow of energy through the system becomes highly inefficient. This is because the Structure component is relatively small, and it is incapable of exerting enough force to drive the remaining components of the system efficiently. Disorder, or what we scientists refer to as entropy, quickly takes over.

If the Processes component is undersized, too much of the energy transferred from the Structure will be consumed by people meeting and talking endlessly about how everything is "supposed to get done," leaving the Culture component with insufficient energy to effectively move the business forward.

If the Culture component is not understood as being the ultimate recipient of energy from Purpose, Strategy, Structure, and Processes, problems in the business will be attributed to its workforce. The people will be seen as disengaged, not committed, and entitled. Effort after effort will be made to fix the people. Little to no effort will be made to fix the system. Fixing a flat tire will still leave you stuck on the side of the road if there is no gas in the car.

The external forces that we discussed earlier in chapter 2 (emerging technology, people preferences, and market fragmentation/consolidation) are constantly demanding adaptive responses from businesses. When a business is operated as a set of independent components rather than as a holistic system, responses tend to be more incremental rather than transformational, because of the siloed nature of the organization.

We now understand that when we say a business must constantly adapt to change, what we are really saying is that its people must constantly adapt to change. To survive and thrive under incredibly stressful internal and external forces, the business must be designed such that transformational change can be achieved by deploying small well-focused actions, avoiding the disruptions to operations associated with larger-scale efforts—a laser rather than a scalpel.

In addition, siloed responses will often unintentionally create new or exacerbate existing destructive relationships among the components. As more actions are implemented to address these negative impacts, more interferences will be created, thus further compromising the operation of the system.

If our business design is both *holistic* (recognizes that the whole is greater than the sum of its parts) and *synergistic* (recognizes that the relationships among the parts have an impact on the whole), we can better foster collaborative problem-solving across functional areas. This gives us an advantage over our competitors who are subject to the same change events, but who operate their businesses according to silos, and therefore create large disruptions to achieve incremental progress when trying to adapt.

In chapter 9, I'll show you the best way I know to get things done efficiently and effectively in a collaborative manner, even when you must cross functional areas to do so.

EFFECTIVENESS OF THE SYSTEM

How do we ensure that *proportional importance* of each component is optimized for business success? We employ what is known as a *Measure of Effectiveness* (*MOE*), which assesses the ability of a system to meet its needs. This measure can be quantitative or qualitative based on your objective. As we discussed in chapter 1, most businesses only apply a quantitative MOE based on monetary metrics.

As you now understand, a business is a system of people, and the only meaningful way to assess its performance is to complement that quantitative, money-focused MOE with a qualitative, people-focused MOE.

How do we do that? We ask questions like the following:

- How effective are we?
- How efficient are we?
- How good is our employee experience?
- What level of value do we provide for our customers?
- How does our community benefit from our being in business?
- What difference are we making?

> An effective business design will facilitate transformational change without large-scale disruptions to operations by creating and maintaining synergy among the design components.

What's Around the Bend

I hope I have convinced you that successfully driving your business forward over an ever-changing landscape requires an intentional design for your Purpose, Strategy, Structure, Processes, and Culture. And that these components do not have an equal impact on the success of the business, so their construct must consider their relative importance. I also hope you can now understand the benefit of viewing your business as one holistic system rather than a collection of parts.

Let me now show you how to optimize each component in the Sprocket design to maximize their impact on the long-term success of your business and create synergies that will facilitate transformational change when needed.

**True optimization
is the revolutionary contribution
of modern research
to decision processes.**

GEORGE DANTZIG

PART 3

Optimizing the Sprocket Design

Turbocharges Your Business

Using sound scientific principles, we developed a more intentional business design for achieving and maintaining long-term success, even during periods of rapid and/or significant change.

The remainder of this book will explain the specific steps you can follow to assess and optimize each of the Sprocket design components in your business. You may be tempted to focus on only one or two components that are your biggest pain points. Don't make that mistake.

Remember, your business is a system, not a set of independent components. If you adjust one component without considering the impacts on the others, you may create more interferences within your operations that will weaken rather than fortify them. To drive up levels of effectiveness, efficiency, and accountability, you want positive, constructive relationships among the components creating synergies.

My recommendation is to work through each of the components sequentially to maximize impact on your operations. This allows you to get the "size" of each component right so that the appropriate amount of energy is transferred to the next component, helping it to do its job effectively and efficiently.

What's Around the Bend

In chapter 9, I'll share with you a foolproof way to implement change in your organization without the usual pushback or procrastination.

In chapters 10 through 14, I'll show you how to maximize the effectiveness of each Sprocket design component so that the resulting synergies created will allow your business to better adapt to changing conditions without sacrificing effectiveness, efficiency, or accountability.

You are about to take your business on a journey to a far, far better place. Don't worry, I'll be riding shotgun with you.

**If you always do
what you've always done,
you'll always get
what you've always got.**

———

HENRY FORD

CHAPTER 9

The 5D Method

A Foolproof Way of Implementing Change

Before we dive into how to optimize each of the Sprocket design components, I'd first like to share with you the most effective and efficient way for affecting change in an organization. I call it the 5D Method, and I guarantee that if you adopt this approach in your organization, you will be amazed not only at how many wheels you get unstuck from the mud but also at how quickly you arrive at superior solutions resulting in lasting changes.

Follow this method to systematically assess and optimize your business Purpose, Strategy, Structure, Processes, and Culture.

D1: Discover

The first step in solving a problem is getting a good handle on where you are versus where you want or need to be. This starts with a process of discovery.

In this phase of the process, you bring together a team of individuals who have the education, experience, and expertise to understand the problem at hand and who can develop an appropriate solution. This means that you exclude those individuals who only have opinions. The gap between solutions derived based on education, experience, and expertise and those derived based on opinion is about as wide as the Grand Canyon. The problem that occurs when people only have opinions is that they mistakenly believe that their proposed solutions are of equal value to those proposed by someone with years or decades of education, experience, and expertise, and they can feel insulted when their solutions are not adopted. Best to not solicit input based on an opinion if there is little probability of your using it.

During the Discover phase, the only job at hand is to ascertain where the organization is, where it needs to be, and a few potential solutions to close the gap. Once this work is completed, this phase is over, and you move on to the next phase.

D2: Discuss

In this phase, the same team that did the work during the Discover phase has open and free discussions (rigorous debates are fine!) to evaluate all proposed solutions that were identified in the Discover phase. There should be no filters applied during this phase. A thorough discussion aimed at arriving at the best solutions that can be *tried* is the goal. Once this work is completed, this phase is over, and you move on to the next phase. *Note:* If you want the team doing their best thinking in these meetings, make them device free. Let's limit information overload here.

D3: Decide

Once all viable solutions identified in the Discover phase have been thoroughly vetted by the team during the Discuss phase, one option is chosen as the best to implement as a *potential* permanent solution. It must be understood by all participants that once the selection is made, everyone needs to get behind it. There can be no dissension once a decision is made. The time to debate is during the Discuss phase—period. Once this work is completed, this phase is over, and you move on to the next phase.

D4: Document

If there is one phase of this process that is more important than the others, this is the one. If your decision is not documented, it is guaranteed that memories will vary among the team as time passes. "I thought we decided X." "No, we definitely decided Y." If you don't document the decision, everyone will be acting on their individual memory of what they think got decided.

More importantly, documenting your decisions will help you determine when you've made the wrong decision *before* it gets implemented. In other words, this is where editing takes place. It is very difficult to edit decisions when they are only arrived at via oral communication. When we talk in group settings, we assume that everyone is dialed in and paying attention. We wrongly assume that everything that was said was heard and understood and will be remembered. This is simply not a good assumption where humans are concerned. Our minds often wander during meetings, as we unintentionally or intentionally process other information related to either work or our personal lives. "What time is that new meeting today?" "What did my wife tell me not to forget this morning?" "What should I have for lunch today?"

By documenting our decisions, we can give everyone another opportunity to ensure that they understand the decision they made. It also allows us to see any errors in logic that were not obvious during the discussion because everyone was ready to wrap up the meeting and get on to the next thing.

D5: Do

This one is kind of obvious, but you'd be surprised at how many solutions are developed that never get implemented. I once worked on a project to develop a ten-year Master Plan for a regional park. After more than a year of work, and endless rounds of discussion among the twenty committee members, the Master Plan was finally completed. When I asked when the implementation would begin, the committee chair said, "Oh, we don't have any money in our budget to do anything for at least the next ten years."

Your goal in using this method is to get from Discover to Do as quickly as possible to determine if your proposed solution is viable and adequate. If not, you'll want to crank through the cycle again with your #2 solution and repeat the cycle until you have solved the problem.

When using this method, each phase should be completed before moving on to the next phase. Always work forward, never backward. The goal is to identify and implement the solutions, not have endless meetings.

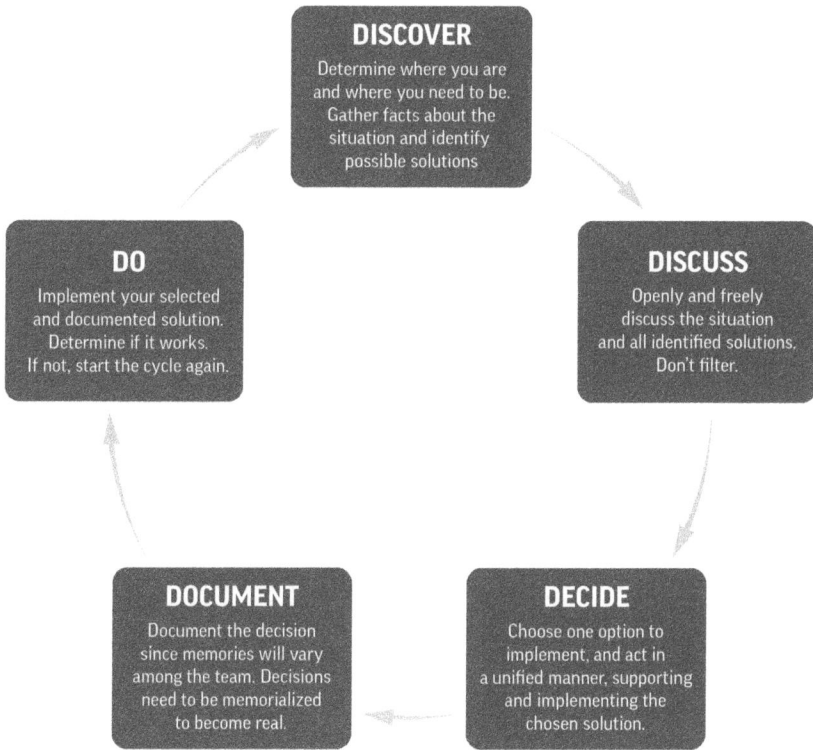

DISCOVER
Determine where you are and where you need to be. Gather facts about the situation and identify possible solutions

DISCUSS
Openly and freely discuss the situation and all identified solutions. Don't filter.

DO
Implement your selected and documented solution. Determine if it works. If not, start the cycle again.

DOCUMENT
Document the decision since memories will vary among the team. Decisions need to be memorialized to become real.

DECIDE
Choose one option to implement, and act in a unified manner, supporting and implementing the chosen solution.

Figure 9.1

Implementing effective change requires a disciplined approach.

What's Around the Bend

In chapters 10 through 14, I'll show you how to optimize each component of the Sprocket business design so that nothing is left to chance in maximizing effectiveness in your organization.

If you don't know where you are going,
any road will get you there.

———

LEWIS CARROLL

CHAPTER 10

Optimizing Your Purpose

Eliminate Confusion

A clear Purpose will help your organization succeed by converting the potential energy contained in the passion of your employees and customers into kinetic energy that drives your business forward.

In chapter 3, you learned that a Purpose statement should convey an organization's commitment to a cause that creates value. To optimize your Purpose, we'll want it to function as a giant magnet, strongly attracting loyal and like-minded customers and employees and forming the basis of all decisions and actions within your organization.

Assessing Your Purpose

Many organizations believe that they have a unifying principle guiding their organization, because they see it on their website, email signature, business card, or letterhead. Here is where the rubber meets the road.

If you have a documented purpose, mission, or vision statement that employees (and you) can state from memory, it inspires them (and you) and clearly conveys both a cause and a value; congratulations! Your organization is truly operating under a guiding statement, no matter what you call it.

If no one can remember or recite it, it is not and cannot drive all your organizational decisions and actions. So, as proud of it as you may be, you must let it go. If you, your employees, or your customers do not feel inspired when reading (or thinking about) your Purpose, it can only serve as a weak magnet incapable of attracting the customers and employees you desire and therefore will only drive your organization as far as the lands of Ho Hum.

Optimizing Your Purpose

If your Purpose is not yet optimized, don't despair. We'll walk through the steps to take in this section that will allow you to develop a clear Purpose statement that is the right one for *your* business.

STEP 1: DEFINE YOUR COMMUNITY

What is the primary group that your organization presently serves?

Many organizations identify the primary group they serve using a descriptor, such as industry, target market, locality, demographic, or niche. These descriptors help categorize or describe the members of the identified group based on some common interests or characteristics that the organization *thinks* might drive their needs and wants.

Once you are clear on the primary group your organization is in business to serve, you'll want to reframe that group as a *community*. The difference between a community and a group of people who share common interests and characteristics is the belief by its members that they are distinct in some meaningful respect from society at large. Members of a community share a self-defined *identity* that sets them apart from others, and you need to discover what that is.

To use your Purpose to effectively communicate that you understand what is important to your community, you must speak their language. If your community is a fun-loving irreverent bunch, you won't connect with them at any meaningful level if you use formal, button-downed language in your Purpose statement. On the contrary, it can be dangerous to try to come off as quirky if you are accountants—no one wants whimsical accountants when dealing with the Internal Revenue Service (IRS).

Your Purpose must be relevant for today and tomorrow. Therefore, you should carefully consider what you think the future holds for the community you choose to serve so that you can follow your community into the future. If your community is likely to shrink in the coming years, you'll need to find ways to increase the value you provide to remain relevant and profitable or start planning to serve a new community.

STEP 2: IDENTIFY YOUR VALUE

Providing value to your chosen community requires an understanding of what is most important to them. It's not enough to know what they want or need; you must understand the *emotions* behind these wants and needs. When parents buy a car for their child, their main concern is safety, because they do not want their child to be hurt or die if they end up in an accident. They will pay more for enhanced safety features in an unconscious attempt to allay their own worry.

Dudley Moore's character in the movie *Crazy People* understood this. Fed up with ads that try to trick buyers, he crafted this ad copy for Volvo cars. "Buy Volvos. They're boxy, but good. We know they're not sexy. This is not a smart time to be sexy anyway, with so many new diseases around. Be safe instead of sexy. Volvo—boxy but good."

The organization does not define the value it provides to their chosen community; the members of their chosen community do. If you want to be perceived as helpful to another person, you need to do things that they find helpful, not things that you think they should find helpful. There is a big difference between the two approaches.

Therefore, it is essential that you listen to what your community is telling you about the value *they believe* your organization is providing to them. There are many ways to listen to what your customers value about your products or services—direct feedback, online reviews, customer service interactions, focus groups, and surveys, just to name a few.

The key is to hear what they are saying and act on that information, because only with their definition of value in mind can your organization align your products and services with the emotions driving their needs or wants. If the value your organization offers is cutting-edge technology, your community should desire innovation over stability. In other words, your target community should not be baby boomers.

Remember, your goal is to meet a need or want in a manner that has real or perceived value to your community. The goal is not to get your community to change its needs or wants or redefine its definition of value according to your standards and perspectives. You want to enter the conversation that is already occurring in the minds of your community members rather than change the conversation. Think of it this way; you don't want to spend your time and resources trying to convince someone they have a headache, so they'll buy your aspirin; you want to find a community of people who have headaches and sell them lots of your aspirin.

A basic tenet with predictable results in political communications is that candidates must define themselves or their opponents will do it for them. It is no different in business. You need to clearly define the value you offer your community in your Purpose statement so that your competitors don't.

STEP 3: CRAFT YOUR PURPOSE STATEMENT

If you currently have some combination of Mission/Vision/Purpose statements and believe they successfully convey both the cause to which your organization is committed and the value that you provide, don't toss them aside. Summarize them in a more concise statement. If they do not adequately articulate your cause and value, you'll save yourself a lot of time and energy if you simply set them aside and start from scratch. If what you have is not serving you, it's best to just acknowledge that and move forward, no matter how attached some may be to these statements.

Let me show you how to create a Purpose statement from scratch. For this example, we'll assume you are about to open a bakery that specializes in cakes.

First, write a simple sentence that identifies what your organization does and for whom. This does not need to be fancy, just factual at this point.

We bake cakes for people who like cakes.

Next, rewrite this sentence adding words that speak to your community's personality and values.

We bake cakes for people who always eat dessert first.

Now, add the value your community finds in your products or services.

We bake decadent cakes for people who always eat dessert first.

Finally, eliminate as many words as possible without losing meaning. Use present tense verbs to convey it is something you are doing now, not some lofty future goal.

Baking decadent cakes for the dessert-first crowd.

As you begin to craft your Purpose statement, keep these thoughts in mind:

- ⚙ Ideally, your Purpose statement should be a single sentence, so it can be remembered by everyone—employees, customers, and shareholders. Avoid buzzwords and trendy business concepts. These dilute your message of value because your statement will feel contrived.

- ⚙ Your Purpose statement should be inspiring. It should have personality. It should convey what your organization wants its community to be as a direct result of the products and/or services it provides. Employees must believe that they can contribute to the Purpose and that their work will matter to others.

- ⚙ Don't define your Purpose just for today; consider what tomorrow looks like.

Once you have gone through a few iterations and think you have the final version, ask yourself the following questions. If you say no to even one of them, keep working at it.

- ⚙ Upon reading this Purpose statement, will our employees be excited about working at our organization?

- ⚙ Upon reading this Purpose statement, will our customers understand and embrace the value we are offering them?

- ⚙ Does our Purpose statement foster an emotional connection between our organization and our most valuable customers?

- ⚙ Is our Purpose statement actionable?

- ⚙ Will employees know what they can do to make our Purpose statement a reality?

> **Your Purpose statement is optimized when it functions as a giant magnet, strongly attracting loyal and like-minded customers and employees, and forms the basis for all decisions and actions in your organization.**

What's Around the Bend

Once you have your Purpose optimized, you are ready for the next leg of your journey, optimizing your Strategy.

The essence of strategy
is choosing what not to do.

———

MICHAEL PORTER

CHAPTER 11

Optimizing Your Strategy

Eliminate Anxiety

A focused Strategy will help your organization succeed by making sure that the appropriate amount of energy goes to the "wheels" of your business to move it forward at any given speed.

In chapter 4, you learned that a Strategy should provide a detailed plan for internal and external value creation. To optimize your Strategy, we'll want it to be focused on your organization's Core Competencies, each of which achieves alignment between the Give and the Get Fingerprints of your most valuable customers.

Assessing Your Strategy

When asked what the Strategy of your business is, if you answer with "organic growth" or "be the (your type of business) of choice in our (geographic area or market sector)" or if you pull out a laundry list of operational initiatives that are titled Strategies and Tactics, you don't have a business Strategy in the Sprocket sense of that term. Only when you have defined the Core Competencies of your organization, and have aligned them with what your most valuable customers are willing to give up to get your Core Competencies, will you have a business Strategy that will drive your business to your desired destination at a speed you can handle.

Optimizing Your Strategy

If your Strategy is not yet optimized, it's OK. We'll walk through the steps to take in this section that will allow you to develop a focused Strategy that is the right one for *your* business.

STEP 1: DEFINE YOUR CORE COMPETENCIES

Make a list of what you believe are the Core Competencies of your organization. Review your list against the criteria we defined in chapter 4 (shown next for convenience) to determine if it is truly a Core Competency. If all criteria are not met, cross it off your list.

- ✪ Meets the need or want within a sustainable market.
- ✪ Reflects the combined education, expertise, and experience of our team members.
- ✪ Has a standard for performance.
- ✪ Has a typical time frame for completion.
- ✪ Pricing is consistent and according to a pricing model.

Next, answer the following questions for each Core Competency still on your list. Give "Yes" answers a score of 3 and "No" answers a score of 1.

- ✪ Do we have trouble meeting the standards for this product/ service?
- ✪ Are time frames for production met consistently?
- ✪ Is the desired profit achieved consistently?

○ Is the production process documented?

○ Is documentation for this Core Competency used for training?

For the competencies that don't earn a perfect score of 15, review whether each can—or even should—be enhanced to meet the criteria. If not, then at the very least your Strategy should not be built around this product or service, and you should consider whether or not it makes good business sense to continue providing it to your customers.

STEP 2: IDENTIFY YOUR MOST VALUABLE CUSTOMERS

Once you are clear on your Core Competencies, your next task is to identify the customers who provide the most value to your organization.

Using your accounting software, create a report or spreadsheet listing the revenue generated by each individual customer or customer category (depending on the specifics of your business) averaged over the last three years.

Using the Pareto Principle as a rule of thumb, determine which group of customers contributed to the majority of your revenue. Don't obsess about the 80–20 aspect of the principle; what is important is identifying the subset of your customers who are contributing the most to your organization.

If you run an advertising firm, you may have individual clients who are that 20 percent contributing 80 percent to your revenue. If, however, you run a health club, you would want to look at either tiers of membership or your different revenue streams for this analysis (e.g., memberships, field rentals, events, classes). It doesn't matter how you approach this analysis; the important point is that you do some sort of analysis that tells you which subset of your customer population you should build your Strategy around.

STEP 3: DEFINE THE PREFERENCES OF
YOUR MOST VALUABLE CUSTOMERS

As we discussed in chapter 4, you want to position your offerings such that they mirror both the Get Fingerprint and the Give Fingerprint of your most valuable customers to the degree practical. The best way to do that is to compare what your customers are looking for with what you are giving them.

For example, you can prepare your own tax returns, use an online provider, or hire a tax accountant. For simple individual returns, you may choose to prepare the return yourself or pay extra for an online service that has a built-in decision tree and electronically files the return for you. For more complex corporate returns, you'd want to hire a tax accountant to ensure you get all allowable deductions and credits permitted according to the latest IRS guidance. In each scenario, you have a preference of how much time, money, and energy you want to expend to get your tax return prepared and a commensurate expectation of what you will receive in return for your investment.

For each Core Competency you identified in Step 1, create a spreadsheet like the one shown next. For each customer type, assign a percentage that reflects how important each item is to your customers in the Them row. Then assign a percentage that reflects what you demand of your customers in the Us row. Since Functional, Social, and Emotional needs comprise their Get Fingerprint, your answers in these columns must total 100. For instance, Functional = 50 percent, Social = 25 percent, and Emotional = 25 percent. The same concept applies to Time, Money, and Energy, since they comprise the Give Fingerprint.

Going back to our tax return example, if you own a tax accounting practice, you might have two categories of clients—those that have simple returns and those that have complex returns. Your intake process is the same for both types of clients and consists of a twenty-page form that they must fill out, with language indicating that you are relying on their information to be complete and correct. Your spreadsheet might look like the following table. The shaded cells indicate where you have misalignment between the experience your clients desire and the experience your firm delivers.

ABC TAX ACCOUNTANTS–CUSTOMER PREFERENCES							
		GET			GIVE		
Customer Type	Point of View	Functional	Social	Emotional	Time	Money	Energy
Simple Returns	Them	90%	0%	10%	5%	90%	5%
	Us	90%	0%	10%	15%	60%	15%
	Difference	0%	0%	0%	-10%	30%	-10%
Complex Returns	Them	80%	0%	20%	10%	80%	10%
	Us	90%	0%	10%	15%	60%	15%
	Difference	-10%	0%	10%	-5%	20%	-5%

Figure 11.1

STEP 4: ENSURE YOUR OFFERINGS MATCH YOUR CUSTOMER PREFERENCES

If there is not close alignment between your offerings and the Get and Give Fingerprints of your most valuable customers, determine what changes you could make to improve the alignment. For instance, the tax accounting practice in our example might consider using a streamlined intake form for the clients with simple returns, presenting instructions in clear and plain language that will be less intimidating and will reduce the time and energy required for them to complete the form. They could then charge slightly more for the service without losing clients.

For the clients with more complex returns, the practice could charge more if they highlighted their goal of getting the highest refund possible without taking any undue risks. Matching your offerings to your customer preferences gives you a lot of options that do not necessarily include lowering your price.

Keep in mind that spreadsheets are good for analyzing data but not as good for presenting conclusions drawn from the analysis. In the following example, anyone can readily see the misalignment allowing them to focus on the solution, not the spreadsheet. Remember, we want to take action based on information, not endlessly collect and analyze information.

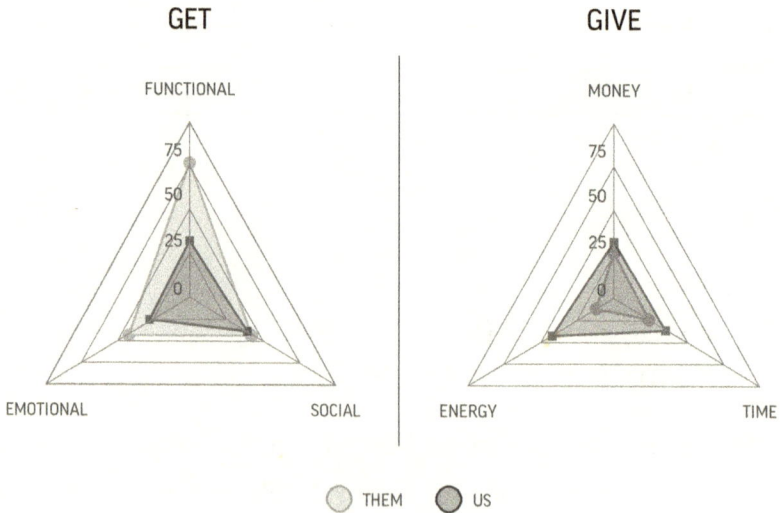

Figure 11.2

> Your Strategy is optimized when it is focused on your organization's Core Competencies, each of which achieves alignment between the Give and Get Fingerprints of your most valuable customers.

What's Around the Bend

Once you have your Strategy optimized, you are ready for the next leg of your journey, optimizing your Structure to facilitate the implementation of your Purpose and Strategy.

Knowledge is not power;

it is only potential.

Applying that knowledge is power.

———

TAKEDA SHINGEN

CHAPTER 12

Optimizing Your Structure

Eliminate Redundancies and Gaps

A solid Structure will help your organization succeed by making sure that the "wheels" of your business get the proper amount of torque so that it can accelerate quickly when needed.

In chapter 5, you learned that a Structure should be designed to optimize performance within and across functional boundaries to maximize internal and external value. To optimize your Structure, we'll want to identify the functional areas of your organization and the responsibilities and accountabilities of each, assess the correct type of knowledge needed for key results, and select the most appropriate method for sharing that knowledge to maximize value for your customers, your employees, and your owners.

Assessing Your Structure

If the Structure of your business is represented by an organizational chart, you don't have a business Structure in the Sprocket sense of that term. Only when you have identified the role of your governing body, defined the functional areas comprising your operations, and ascertained both the types of knowledge each functional area requires and how you can best share that knowledge, will you have a business Structure that will allow your business to accelerate at will.

Optimizing Your Structure

If your Structure is not yet optimized, take a breath, and keep reading. In this section, we'll walk through the steps that will allow you to develop a solid Structure that is the right one for *your* business.

STEP 1: DIAGRAM YOUR STRUCTURE

Wait! Wasn't chapter 5 all about not using an organizational chart to communicate the structure of a business? No. That chapter was all about going beyond the traditional organizational chart. Having a simple graphic of the functional areas in your business is helpful for your employees to see the big picture—initially.

To diagram your structure, you will first need to identify the functional areas of your organization. Be sure to include its owners, governing body, production, sales, and support.

In the following example, Sales is called Business Development. Don't get hung up on labels; just make sure you account for all the functional areas in your organization.

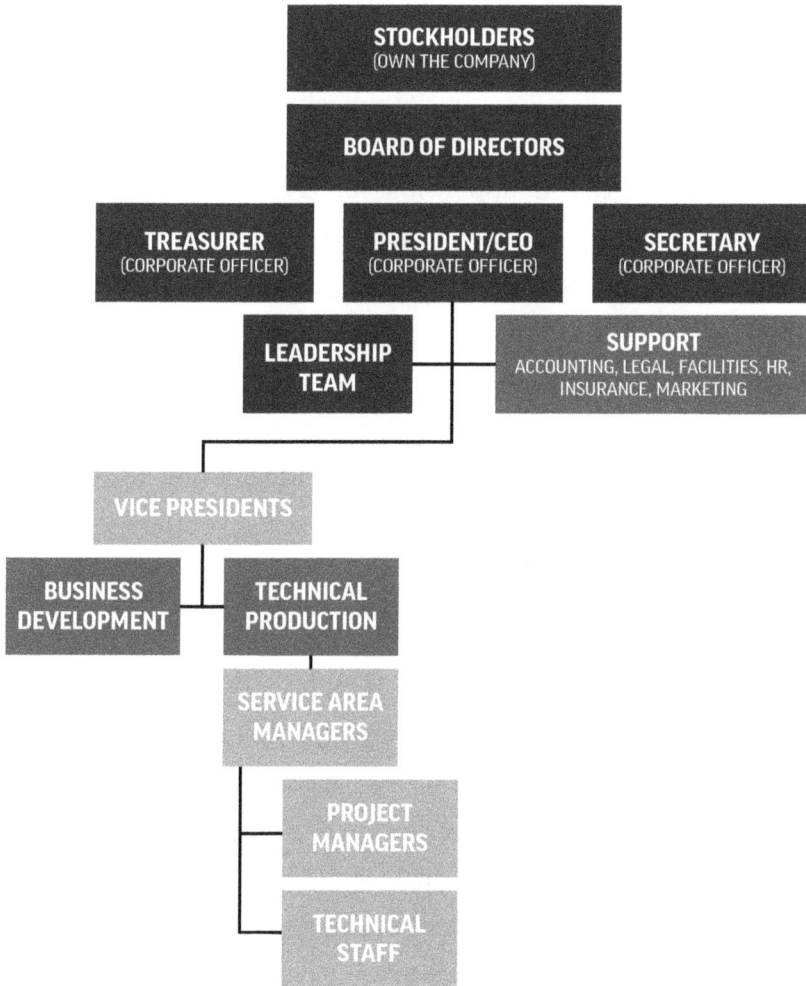

Figure 12.1

STEP 2: ANNOTATE YOUR STRUCTURE DIAGRAM

If you want your employees to really understand what gets done in your organization and by whom, you'll want to annotate your structure diagram with high-level responsibility statements for each functional area to flesh out what that area is responsible and accountable for. For example, such a statement for the leadership team in the diagram might read as follows:

Leadership Team
The leadership team is responsible for (1) defining the purpose, core values, strategy, and structure of the company; (2) developing company-wide policies, processes, and procedures; (3) ensuring all employees follow company-wide policies, processes, and procedures; (4) approving service area–specific policies, processes, and procedures; and (5) developing any company-wide monetary rewards and/or performance-based accountability programs. The leadership team reports directly to the president/CEO.

STEP 3: DEVELOP AUTHORITY MATRICES

Although publishing an annotated structure diagram is an effective means of communicating to all your employees how the business is structured and why, a different tool is needed within functional areas to provide basic guidelines around decision-making boundaries so that all employees in the functional area understand clearly what is in and what is out of their decision-making purview. The best tool for this purpose is the Authority Matrix.

This tool is a simple table used to identify the high-level responsibilities and accountabilities assigned to a functional area and all the roles operating within the functional area. Within the body of the table, each role is identified as a Doer (Responsible), Approver (Accountable), Participator, or none of those. Roles that only participate *can* provide input or guidance, but they are *not* tasked with making decisions themselves.

There is only one hard-and-fast rule in constructing an effective Authority Matrix: only *one* role can be designated as the Approver (Accountable) for any given decision.

Done correctly, a simple one-page Authority Matrix can save untold hours of meetings and emails within a functional area by making clear who decides what—proactively.

HUMAN RESOURCES AUTHORITY MATRIX			
A=ACCOUNTABLE/ APPROVES	D=DOES/DECIDES	P=PARTICIPATES (INPUT, GUIDANCE, INFORMED)	
PRESIDENT/CEO	OFFICE MANAGER	VICE PRESIDENTS	SERVICE AREA MANAGERS
COMPENSATION & BENEFITS			
Develops Compensation Matrix Annually	A	P	P	
Allocates Billable, Nonbillable, and Leave Hours Based on Break Even and Target Analyses Annually	A	P	P	
Calculates Team and Individual Reviews Annually		P	P	
Determines Benefits Package Annually	A	P		
Maintains Time Off Vision Project Plans		D		
Facilitates Open Enrollment Process and New Hire Benefits Selection		D		
Generates Total Annual Compensation Reports for Employees Annually		D		
TRAINING & DEVELOPMENT			
Prepares Annual Budget and Plan for Professional Development of Service Area Team Members		P	D	P
Conducts Organizational Orientation for New Hires		D	P	P
Conducts Service Area Orientation for New Hires			P	D
Monitors Implementation of Professional Development Activities of All Employees		D	P	P
Conducts Performance Appraisals of Service Team Members Annually		P	P	D
Tracks Training Certifications, Registrations and Licenses of All Employees		D	P	P
Proactively Communicates Pending Expiration of Certifications, Registrations and Licenses to All Employees		D	P	P
Maintains Career Flow and Position Descriptions Content for Service Area		P	P	D
SAFETY			
Manages Company Safety Program	A	D	P	P
Schedules and Coordinates Company-Wide Safety Training		D	P	P
Obtains All Required Employee Security Clearances		D	P	P

Figure 12.2

STEP 4: DETERMINE THE KNOWLEDGE TYPE NEEDED

In this step, you are going to determine the primary type of knowledge required by each functional area to provide its internal or external products or services. As we discussed in chapter 5, the goal of the Structure is to design your organization with an eye toward maximizing value for both customers and the organization. By determining the predominant type of knowledge used in each functional area, you can ensure that it is in alignment with the value of the products that the customers (whether internal or external) of that functional area receive. In addition, you can maximize value to the organization by ensuring that all employees in a functional area have all the knowledge required to be successful in their work, thereby driving up effectiveness, efficiency, and accountability.

To identify the primary type of knowledge required in any functional area, answer the following five questions, and assign the score indicated for the answer you select. Then, total the scores to determine the composite Knowledge Type score for that functional area.

Knowledge Type Questionnaire

Which statement best describes the primary work the group performs for internal or external customers?

- ❖ routine tasks that require basic knowledge (1)
- ❖ intermediate tasks that require intermediate knowledge (5)
- ❖ innovative tasks that require advanced knowledge (10)

Which statement best describes the problems employees of the group encounter when performing their work?

- ❖ low impact, high occurrence of standard variety (1)
- ❖ medium impact, high occurrence of standard variety with occasional unusual variety (5)

⚙ high impact, high occurrence of unusual variety (10)

Which is the primary type of knowledge employees of the group rely on when performing their work?

⚙ implicit (experience-based, undocumented, difficult to share/teach) (10)

⚙ explicit (skills-based, documented, easy to share/teach) (1)

Which best describes the employee-to-manager ratio for the group?

⚙ low (less than five employees to one manager) (10)

⚙ medium (five to fifteen employees to one manager) (5)

⚙ high (more than fifteen employees to one manager) (1)

Which is the primary method of knowledge sharing within the group?

⚙ people-to-documents (system that codifies and disseminates through documents) (1)

⚙ people-to-people (system of verbally or physically training/mentoring) (10)

A Knowledge Type score of <10 indicates that the predominant knowledge type needed by the functional area is *procedure*.

A Knowledge Type score of 10–30 indicates that the predominant knowledge type needed by the functional area is *experience*.

A Knowledge Type score of >30 indicates the predominant knowledge type needed by the functional area is *expertise*.

STEP 5: DETERMINE THE VALUE OF THE PRODUCTS

Whether the products created by a functional area are for internal or external customers, you will maximize value to them if the primary knowledge type used in that functional area is aligned with the product type this functional area is tasked with creating.

To identify the value of the products created by any functional area, answer the following four questions, and assign the score indicated for the answer you select. Then, total the scores to determine the composite Value Position score for that functional area.

Product Value Questionnaire

The value of primary products or services in this functional area is

- low (1)
- medium (5)
- high (10)

Which statement best describes the primary products or services of this functional area?

- very common in our industry (1)
- somewhat common in our industry (5)
- one-of-a-kind, can't get it anywhere else (10)

The profit obtained from the primary products or services of the functional area is

- low (1)
- medium (5)
- high (10)

The best word to describe the work performed in this functional area is

- commoditized (1)
- systematized (5)
- customized (10)

A Value Position score of <10 indicates that the primary products or services of this functional area belong in the *commodity* category.

A Value Position score of 10–30 indicates that the primary products or services of this functional area belong in the *standard* category.

A Value Position score of >30 indicates that the primary products or services of this functional area belong in the *custom* category.

STEP 6: COMPARE YOUR KNOWLEDGE TO VALUE

Now that you have determined the Knowledge Type needed for a given functional area and have determined the Value Position of what this group produces, you need to determine if the knowledge is aligned with the value, and if not, make the necessary adjustments. It may be helpful to create two graphs to better see the comparison of your scores.

KNOWLEDGE TO VALUE BALANCE

YOUR KNOWLEDGE TYPE SCORE

36.2

0   40

YOUR VALUE POSITION SCORE

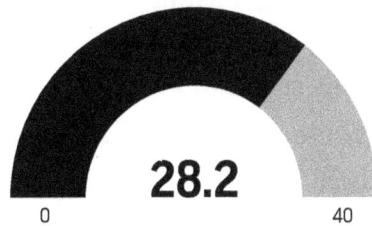

28.2

0   40

Figure 12.3

In this example, the Knowledge Type score indicates that this company *thinks* its team requires knowledge at the high end of the Expertise range. And yet, its Value Position score indicates that this group produces Standard products. Thus, there is a misalignment between the knowledge needed and the value produced. Because this company is overestimating the knowledge the group requires to successfully accomplish their work, it likely has highly paid employees who are overqualified for their position. This company would be better served by documenting how their standard products are best produced and training a team capable of executing these processes to a high level of competency.

Imbalances between the kind of knowledge your team needs to produce and the value of that product must be addressed.

STEP 7: SHARING KNOWLEDGE

After aligning the Knowledge Type and Value Positions within your functional area, the last step in optimizing your Structure is making sure that knowledge is being *shared* so that it can be used effectively and efficiently.

To do so, answer the following two questions separately for each functional area. Use the score indicated for the answer you select for each question. Then, total the scores to determine the composite Knowledge Sharing score for that functional area.

Knowledge Sharing Questionnaire

We use information and communication technologies to reduce the cost of *acquiring* knowledge.

- ✿ strongly disagree (1)
- ✿ disagree (2)
- ✿ neutral (5)
- ✿ agree (9)
- ✿ strongly agree (10)

We use information and communication technologies to reduce the cost of *communicating* knowledge.

- ✿ strongly disagree (1)
- ✿ disagree (2)
- ✿ neutral (5)
- ✿ agree (9)
- ✿ strongly agree (10)

A Knowledge Sharing score of <5 is appropriate if the functional area is relying primarily on *expertise* knowledge to perform its work.

A Knowledge Sharing score of 5–15 is appropriate if the functional area is relying primarily on *experience* knowledge to perform its work.

A Knowledge Sharing score of >15 is appropriate if the functional area is relying primarily on *procedure* knowledge to perform its work.

If your use of these technologies is not aligned with the knowledge demands of your functional areas, you are investing either too little or too much in them. Either practice negatively impacts performance of the functional area.

Where needed, increase or decrease the use of information and communication technologies to optimize knowledge sharing commensurate with the needs of the functional area.

Once finalized, changes to your new Structure should only be undertaken when the size or complexity of your organization significantly increases/decreases or the organization enters a new stage of maturity. Don't be tempted to fiddle with the design.

> **Your Structure is optimized when it identifies the functional areas of your organization and the responsibilities and accountabilities of each, assesses the correct type of knowledge needed for key results, and selects the most appropriate method for sharing that knowledge to maximize value for your customers, your employees, and your owners.**

What's Around the Bend

Once you have your Structure optimized, you are ready for the next leg of your journey, optimizing your Processes to achieve the core functions of your organization effectively and efficiently.

I hear and I forget.

I see and I remember.

I do and I understand.

———

CONFUCIUS

CHAPTER 13

Optimizing Your Processes

Eliminate Frustration

Effective and efficient Processes will help your organization succeed by allowing the "wheels" of your business to turn at different speeds, so you successfully negotiate the unexpected curves in the road along your journey.

In chapter 6, you learned that business Processes (rules, policies, processes, and procedures) should provide a road map for conducting day-to-day operations by guiding decision-making, streamlining workflows, and maximizing the quality of outcomes produced. To optimize your Processes, we'll want them to minimize mistakes, maximize delegation, make productivity effective and efficient, and drive up levels of accountability in all levels of your organization.

Assessing Your Processes

If your business Processes consist only of content-dense policy-ish documents, you don't have Processes in the Sprocket sense of that term. Only when you have distinguished between rules, policies, processes, and procedures and have created simple documents that are easily accessible by all employees to help them be successful in their work, will you have business Processes that will allow your business to confidently negotiate every hairpin curve it encounters.

Now, before we get into the steps you need to follow to optimize your Processes, let's consider a simple example to review the different functions for each of these various documents that comprise business Processes.

Let's say your organization is a community bank. Federal regulators determine the maximum dollar amount that the bank can lend to a given borrower, expressed as a percentage of the bank's capital (external rule). The bank can set its own limits on individual lending limits, provided they are less than those specified by the regulators (internal rule). The bank sets limits on the concentration of loans in certain market sectors, such as commercial real estate (policy). Individual loan officers at the bank must evaluate the creditworthiness of a customer and present their assessment to the loan committee (process). Once a loan is approved, documents must be prepared, shared, and stored according to strict protocols (procedure).

Optimizing Your Processes

If your Processes are not yet optimized, Sprocket's got you covered. Let's walk through the steps that will allow you to develop a series of effective and efficient Processes that are the right ones for *your* business.

STEP 1: DEFINE YOUR RULES

As we discussed in chapter 6, every organization is subject to laws and regulations imposed by local, state, and federal governments to create and keep order, protect property, provide a sense of fair play, and keep people safe. It is through an organization's rules that employees understand the laws and regulations they must abide by and any internal codes of conduct that must be adhered to.

The most effective way to communicate all laws, regulations, and internal rules that apply to your organization is to develop a *Compliance Code*. The main messages to communicate in this document are as follows:

- ⚙ The laws and regulations that apply to the organization and its employees;
- ⚙ the organization's commitment to complying with the letter and intent of these laws and regulations;
- ⚙ the internal rules of the organization;
- ⚙ the organization's expectation that *all* employees, owners, officers, and directors will comply with external and internal rules to limit unnecessary risk to the organization, employees, customers, vendors, and guests;
- ⚙ the result of noncompliance for each rule; and
- ⚙ the reporting process for *Compliance Code* violations.

STEP 2: RANK YOUR FUNCTIONAL AREAS

After creating your *Compliance Code*, you need to ensure that you have the appropriate catalog of Policy, Process, and Procedure documents for each functional area within your organization. Using the Authority Matrices that you created for each functional area after reading chapter 12, score each listed critical function according to how well the team is executing on these functions (i.e., achieving the desired outcome). Use something simple like a scale of 1–5; or A–D; or Green, Yellow, Red. Keep it simple and don't overthink it.

Based on the composite score for each functional area, rank your functional areas from most effective to least effective. Starting with the least effective functional area, follow the remaining steps, and then repeat with each sequential functional area, moving from least effective to most effective.

STEP 3: DEFINE YOUR POLICIES

Remember, policies are best reserved for providing *guidance* on decision-making under various circumstances to ensure uniformity in the ultimate decision being made. Policies do not convey rules.

Determine whether you have an effective policy for any common decisions that need to be made in this functional area. For those decisions that you determine do not have an effective policy to effectively guide the decision-making process, create the needed policy.

STEP 4: DEFINE YOUR PROCESSES

Determine whether you have an effective process for any common actions that need to be taken in this functional area. Remember that a process defines the high-level view of tasks that need to be performed to achieve an objective, the order in which they are best performed, who performs them, and who is accountable for their successful completion. The distinction between policies and processes is that the latter have a start and end with distinct steps in between.

Rather than content-dense process documents, consider creating process diagrams. Process diagrams are a great alternative to text-based process documents because they graphically illustrate workflows, and as we all know, a picture is better than reading one thousand words. Lengthy process documents are fine as reference materials, but if that is all you offer your employees, you run the risk that the documents won't be read, making your painstakingly crafted documents all but useless.

Here are a few ways process diagrams can be more effective than written documents:

- They allow the user to see the entire process from start to finish on one page.
- They eliminate inconsistencies that are typically buried in the details of the text.
- They promote coordination, collaboration, and empowerment because they show the interactions among positions in the department.
- They provide better visibility into operations, allowing quick and easy identification of gaps and redundancies that need to be addressed.
- When changes are needed (and they will be needed), they allow rapid communication of the changes to the team with minimal confusion.

To create an effective process diagram, follow these simple steps. Note that although you certainly can build the diagram showing every finite task and decision point, it is best to keep process diagrams to one page wherever possible. Details can be filled in with Procedure documents. Remember, the goal is to have a simple picture of the entire workflow, not an overly complex one.

- Define the overall objective of the process and what a successful outcome would look like.
- Break down the process needed to achieve the overall objective into macroscale phases.

⚙ For each macroscale phase of the process, identify all tasks that must be accomplished in that phase. Do not be concerned with who accomplishes the task at this point, just what needs to be done and in what order. Use verbs to start the task description (e.g., revise, draft, perform). Use consistent shapes to differentiate elements in the process (e.g., squares for tasks, diamonds for decisions, ovals for start/stop points).

⚙ Assign each task to *the lowest employee competency level* required. This will require thinking through which tasks each position within the functional area can successfully perform with little to no additional guidance.

⚙ Ensure that all needed review is included as distinct tasks within the process. This step shines a bright light on where there is too little (or too much) oversight. Managers who over-delegate will have too little oversight, and managers who under-delegate (micromanage) will have too much. Both have negative impacts on effectiveness and efficiency of the process and on the confidence of the team members. Making these decisions is where clarity really happens about *who* is doing *what* and *why*.

⚙ Color-code the activity boxes by position to allow team members to easily see their role in the workflow. Use contrasting colors to make this as visually distinct as possible.

⚙ Refine the diagram until you have the right tasks in the right order to accomplish the desired objective, where each activity is an action performed by one position.

⚙ Finally, add arrows to clarify the workflow direction.

Once the complete flow of tasks has been diagramed for the entire process, stop, and get feedback from actual users. Be sure to get feedback all the way down the line. More senior employees may be too far removed from the best way to accomplish lower-level tasks, but that may not stop them from weighing in on how they think it should be performed.

With all feedback gathered, create a RACI matrix to clarify roles fulfilled by internal and external resources involved in the process and to ensure that internal delegation of authority (empowerment) is maximized. RACI is an acronym (responsible, accountable, consulted, and informed), indicating potential role assignment for a given task.

Although an Authority Matrix assigns responsibility for activities and decisions at the big-picture or 30,000-foot level, a RACI matrix can be used to clarify activities and decisions at the detailed 10,000-foot level.

- For each task/decision, identify the one role (internal or external) that performs the task ("R" = Responsible).

- Identify the one role (internal or external) that approves the task ("A" = Accountable). In most cases, the role that is responsible is also accountable. Exceptions occur when one role performs a task, but a different role must grant final approval.

- Identify all roles (internal or external) that must be consulted before a task is performed ("C" = Consulted). Here, less is more.

- Identify all roles (internal or external) that must be informed after a task has been accomplished ("I" = Informed). Here, less is also more.

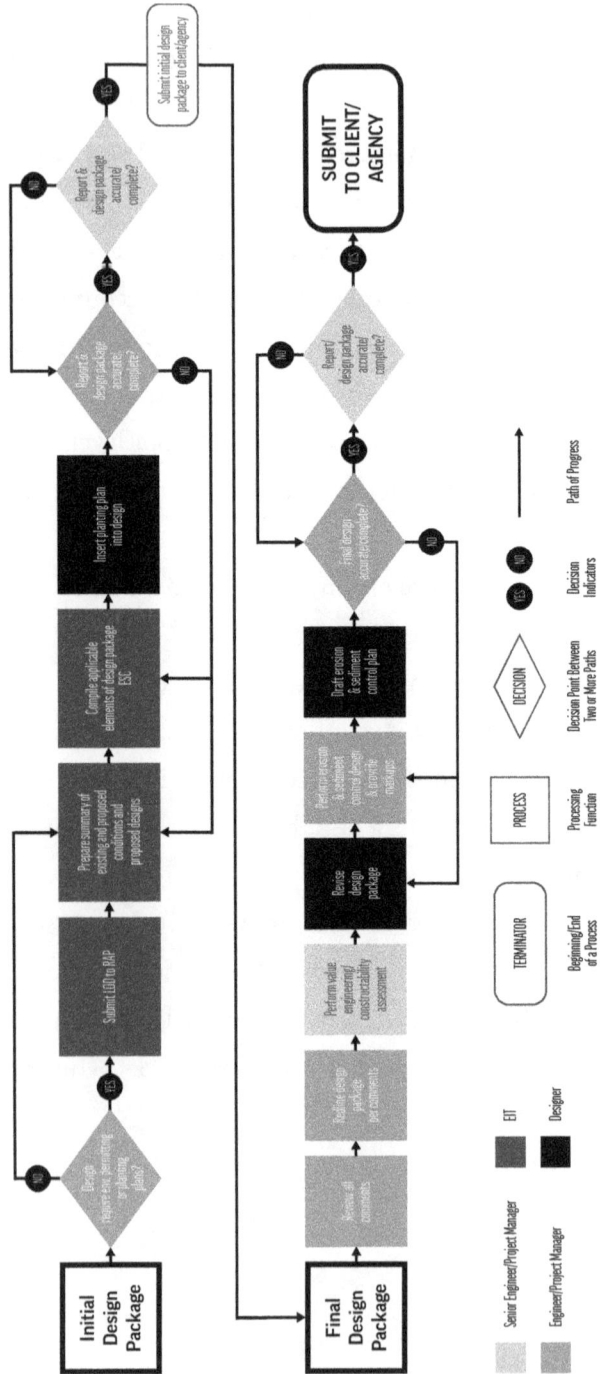

Figure 13.1

RACI DEFINITIONS **R:** WHO IS RESPONSIBLE **A:** WHO IS ACCOUNTABLE **C:** WHO IS CONSULTED **I:** WHO IS INFORMED		TEAM MEMBERS			EXTERNAL RESOURCES			
	D/VP/SVP	SR. ENV. SCIENTIST/PM/QP	ENV. SCIENTIST	STAFF SCIENTIST	PRIME	CLIENT	SUBCONSULTANTS	VENDORS
KICK-OFF MEETING								
Review work plan digital folder		R/A						
Review project plan in vision		R/A						
Select project team members		R/A						
Review with D/VP/SVP	C/A	R						
Schedule kick-off meeting	I	R/A	I	I				
Conduct kick-off meeting with team		R/A						
AGENCY ASSESSMENT REQUESTS								
Request vicinity maps & shapefiles from GEO			R/A					
Confirm vicinity maps are accurate/complete			R/A					
Prepare/submit agency assessment requests				R/A				
Review/store agency response			R/A					
Determine if agencies have issues			R/A					
Discuss project implications with client			R/A			I	I	
Submit agency responses to client			R/A					

Figure 13.2

- Review the RACI matrix to identify the following imbalances and make the suggested adjustments to improve the process.
- Roles with many "R"s: Do these positions have too much work? Can this work be rebalanced among the team?
- Tasks/Decisions with many "R"s: Are there too many roles involved in the process?
- Roles with many "A"s: Can the authority be pushed down to another level within the team?

- Tasks/Decisions with many "C"s: Do all these roles really need to be consulted, or is this just unnecessarily slowing down progress?

- Tasks/Decisions with many "I"s: Do all these roles really need to be informed? You do not need to, nor do you want to, list everyone who might have a passing interest in the progress of the task. The role of "I"s should only be used to indicate when the baton is being handed off from one role to another to allow the next step in the process to be initiated.

Now, transfer the assignments made in creating the RACI matrix to your process diagram.

- Have the default protocol be that any role assigned a task/decision is both Responsible and Accountable, thus requiring no annotation of these activity boxes. For exceptions where one role performs the task but another role grants final approval of the work, add the letter "R" to the task box and the letter "A" to the approval box.

- Wherever other roles are consulted in the process, add a box with the letter "C" and list all roles who are consulted at that point in the process. Be discerning here.

- Wherever other roles are informed in the process, add a box with the letter "I" and list all roles who are informed at that point in the process. Also, be discerning here.

Retain the original RACI matrix as a separate document. When conditions change, use the matrix to illustrate both current responsibility assignments and proposed future assignments to facilitate discussions and decisions among the team about how to best respond to these changes. Once the changes are agreed to, the process diagram can be quickly and easily updated.

STEP 5: DEFINE YOUR PROCEDURES

We talked about this in detail in chapter 6, but it bears repeating: procedures define the detailed steps required to perform the tasks identified in the process diagram. Process is the big picture, and procedures are the details of that picture. Too often, procedures are not given the importance they deserve because "everyone already knows how to do it." But knowing "how to do it" does not mean everyone is "doing it" the same way, every time, in the most efficient and effective method.

For each process diagram, determine whether you have the requisite procedure documents to support it. Where the answer is no, create the needed procedure documents. The best format for procedure documents is a checklist, which allows employees to complete procedures using the instructional tool. Remember, not every activity requires a procedure document. For instance, if a required task is to complete a form, and the form has explicit instructions on how to complete it printed on the form, a procedure document is not needed.

After developing a draft procedure document, answer these three critical questions to ensure that you will optimize the output you desire.

- ⚙ Does the procedure work *under ideal or controlled conditions?* This question addresses the concept of *efficacy.*
- ⚙ Does the procedure work well *under real-world conditions* in your organization? This question addresses the concept of *effectiveness.*
- ⚙ Is it working in the *most economical way* in terms of time, energy, or money? This question addresses the concept of *efficiency.*

Once you create a draft procedure, make sure it can achieve the desired result, even if it requires specific conditions. Then, test it in a real-world environment. If found to be effective, do what you reasonably can to make it more economical.

STEP 6: MAKE YOUR DOCUMENTS ACCESSIBLE

To make sure you get a return on the investment of time and energy you devoted to creating a complete catalog of Policies, Processes, and Procedures for your organization, these documents must be readily accessible to your employees.

To communicate how important Policies, Processes, and Procedures are in supporting the Purpose and Strategy of your organization, it is helpful to create a guidance document that relays how each of these documents is used throughout your organization. Be sure to explain what precipitates changes in these documents, how changes will be communicated, and how changes will be implemented. Linking these documents to your Purpose and Strategy helps employees take ownership of their individual contribution to your organization's success.

You'll want to consider developing a *cataloging* and *classification* system for these documents. Cataloging is a compiled list of documents so that employees know what is available. Classification provides a means of bringing all documents on the same subject together in one place. These two steps facilitate easy access to the documents and enhance their effective utilization.

Depending on the size of your organization, you may want to catalog all Policies, Processes, and Procedures for the entire organization, but classify based on department. This approach allows the employees of the accounting department, for example, to easily access and use their documents without having to wade through the human resources department documents.

The goal is to make it as easy as possible for employees to find up-to-date documents relevant to their role/department so that they can follow the proper steps rather than try to remember them all or decide to wing it because it's too much trouble to look up.

Don't make the mistake of thinking because your employees read your documents once, they've committed everything to memory. Be sure to provide ongoing training in the content and use of these documents. The more familiar you make your employees with your documents through regular training, the higher the probability they will use them correctly and consistently.

Finally, incorporate the use of these documents into your professional development and performance management processes. Rewarding your employees for simply following your Policies, Processes, and Procedures is a great practice because the proper use of these documents has a direct and significant bearing on your organization's success.

○ ○ ○

Let's consider the Widget Company that manufactures one, and only one, type of widget. They use a color-coded process diagram to map out their unique process for producing this widget on their factory floor. New employees are given a small version of this diagram in their orientation so that they can become familiar with not only their role in the process of manufacturing the widget but everyone else's role too. Procedure documents that provide detailed instructions for operating each machine in the process are kept in three-ring binders adjacent to each machine. The manufacturing process is performed in accordance with the company's clear commitment to safety, which is spelled out in their detailed safety policies that drive the training each employee receives on a regular basis.

> **Your Processes (rules, policies, processes, and procedures) are optimized when mistakes are minimized, delegation is maximized, productivity is effective and efficient, and accountability is high at all levels of your organization.**

What's Around the Bend

Once you have your Processes optimized, you are ready for the final leg of your journey, optimizing your Culture to provide the proper incentives for your employees to help fulfill your organization's Purpose.

No company, small or large,

can win over the long run

without energized employees

who believe in the mission

and understand how to achieve it.

—

JACK WELCH

CHAPTER 14

Optimizing Your Culture

Eliminate Lackluster Results

As we discussed in chapter 7, a harmonious business Culture is automatically achieved when the organization's Purpose, Strategy, Structure, and Processes are optimized. But, as I also hinted in that same chapter, an organization can transform a harmonious culture into a fantastically harmonious one if it is willing to consider adding a few additional elements that turbocharge the intrinsic motivators of its employees and limit the use of extrinsic motivators.

As a reminder, a fantastically harmonious culture is one where every employee could honestly say, "I know what this organization is trying to accomplish. I know exactly how my work fits into the big picture here. I have the guidance I need to do my work at a high level without the need to guess or constantly ask questions of my supervisor. I know which behaviors are valued and rewarded, and I feel aligned with those values."

Motivation Turbocharger 1: Career Development

A group of employees may exhibit wonderful teamwork, find constructive solutions to internal conflict, and feel individually empowered. Unfortunately, if these employees do not see a clear road map for individual career development and advancement, it will be a challenge to retain them over the long term.

To be effective, this road map must contain the following two critical components. These, of course, are meant to complement a solid Structure for the organization that outlines its critical functions.

- *What I Must Know:* A well-defined career path within their department that identifies all positions available in that department, the specific competencies expected of employees in each position, and the average time required to gain full competency in each position.

- *What I Must Do:* Position descriptions for every position available within their department explaining the primary role of each position within that department, the primary responsibilities of each position, and how much time should typically be spent on each responsibility.

CAREER PATH (WHAT I MUST KNOW)

The best way to communicate a career path is with a diagram. Ideally, this diagram should illustrate the progression of positions within the department and the locations of any career *confluence* and career *divergence* points that occur along the way.

A career confluence point is where employees can *add* a new, separate, and distinct role in addition to their primary role. A career divergence point is where employees can *leave* their current primary role and embark upon another. The idea is to convey a journey with multiple options so that employees understand that their exact path can be unique to them and does not have to be a one-size-fits-all.

To accomplish this, I developed Career Flows™, where the career path is represented by a flowing stream, communicating continuous movement forward within a given position and between successive positions within a department. This approach contrasts with other conventions showing advancement as a series of discreet landing spots much like a subway map.

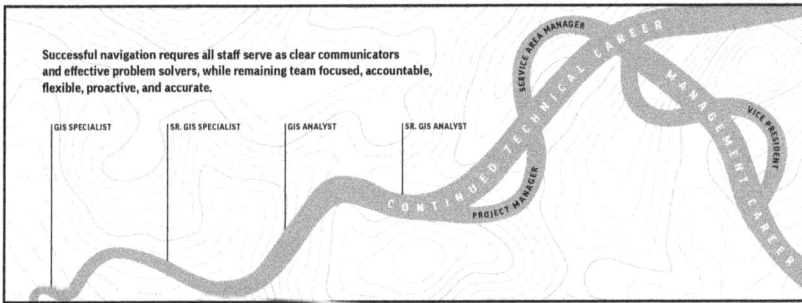

GIS SPECIALIST: Data Collection, Geodatabases. Full Competency (2) 2 Years (2)		LVL 1	LVL 2	LVL 3	LVL 4
	Raster Data Sets & Catalogs	○			
	Mosaic Data Sets	○			
	Vector Data Types	○			
	Vector Data Manipulation	○			
	Tabular Data Sources	○			
	Tabular Data Manipulation	○			
	Tabular Data Calculations & Queries	○			
	Datums, Projections, and Coordinate Systems	○			

SENIOR GIS SPECIALIST: Data Transformation, Data Analysis, Full Competency: Additional 3 Years (5)		LVL 1	LVL 2	LVL 3	LVL 4
	Data Import/Export	○			
	Data Conversion & Transformation	○			
	Spatial ETL Workflows	○			
	Annotation Management		○		
	Geometry Analysis			○	
	Network Analysis			○	
	Spatial Analysis				○

Figure 14.1

Where another role is assumed in addition to the primary role (such as a senior GIS analyst also functioning as a project manager in this example), the additional role is shown as a separate smaller channel flowing adjacent to the mainstream channel. Where employees can choose a new career path (such as moving from a technical role to a management role in this example), a fork in the mainstream channel is shown. This graphical representation allows all employees to quickly see the various options for advancement and chart their own course. The organization creates the path; employees chart their journey along that path.

You'll want a separate Career Flow™ for each department in your organization. To build one, follow these easy steps:

- Define the departmental positions with an eye toward progression of knowledge needed to allow employees to move from one position to another.

- Define the specific competencies required for each position with an eye toward skill building to allow employees to grow within each position.

- It is helpful to approach developing the competency requirements for each position as one would if developing a curriculum for a college degree. For instance, to take a high school graduate and have that student graduate in four years with an engineering degree, you must identify all the concepts that must be learned to demonstrate mastery of the discipline. You must then develop the progression of learning to ensure that basic concepts provide the foundation for more complex concepts (e.g., Introduction to Engineering must be mastered before Comprehensive Design II).

    I recommend four progressive levels (think freshman, sophomore, junior, and senior). These progressive levels allow supervisors to promote employees horizontally, assuring employees move forward within their current position, without the risk of promotion to the next position without necessary skills for success.

These levels also clearly communicate that both horizontal and vertical promotions are based on *mastering* competencies, not elapsed time.

○ To each position, determine the average time required for the average person with the requisite education to master all competencies.

This tenure guide helps employees set realistic expectations for career advancement and helps more driven employees set stretch goals. In addition, it helps your supervisors see when employees are stuck in positions below their capabilities, leading to boredom and perhaps leaving the organization.

The use of Career Flows™ is a superior approach to communicating required skills and competencies for any position and for assessing where employees are along the mastery spectrum for these skills and competencies.

In combination with a *skill development assessment chart*, the use of Career Flows™ helps supervisors determine whether an employee has truly mastered a given competency. A box on the Career Flow™ would *only* be checked if the supervisor sees that the employee is operating at either Stage 3 (Conscious Competence) or Stage 4 (Unconscious Competence).

SKILL DEVELOPMENT

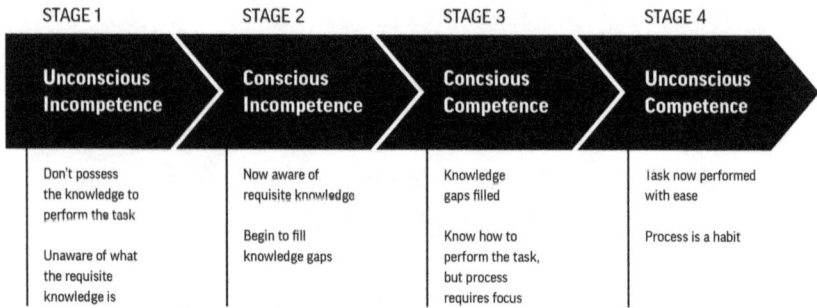

STAGE 1	STAGE 2	STAGE 3	STAGE 4
Unconscious Incompetence	**Conscious Incompetence**	**Concsious Competence**	**Unconscious Competence**
Don't possess the knowledge to perform the task Unaware of what the requisite knowledge is	Now aware of requisite knowledge Begin to fill knowledge gaps	Knowledge gaps filled Know how to perform the task, but process requires focus	Task now performed with ease Process is a habit

Figure 14.2

This approach allows the supervisor to *show* the employee where they are in the progression of the position and helps the employee better understand what they need to do to move forward. This demonstrates to employees that they have accountability for their own career development, eliminating the passive model of career development prevalent in so many organizations. In other words, it supercharges their intrinsic motivation to advance in their career.

Note: Since administrative and management roles represent a wide variety of disciplines (e.g., HR, IT, marketing, accounting), you may find it more helpful to define positions based on progressive levels of independence in their work rather than on specific skills. For these positions, the focus is on how much authority is *delegated* for a given responsibility.

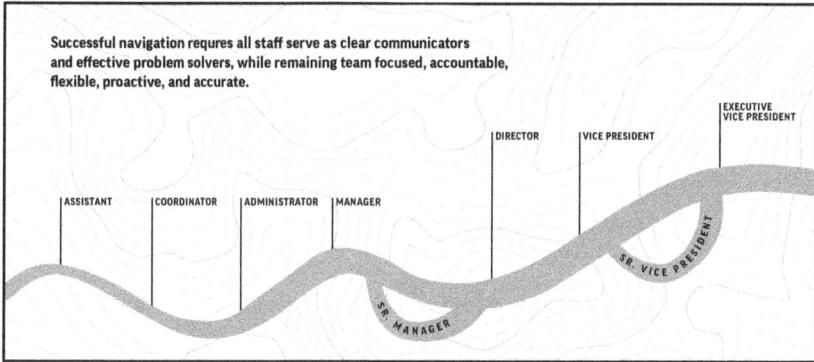

Successful navigation requres all staff serve as clear communicators and effective problem solvers, while remaining team focused, accountable, flexible, proactive, and accurate.

EXECUTIVE VICE PRESIDENT

DIRECTOR   VICE PRESIDENT

ASSISTANT   COORDINATOR   ADMINISTRATOR   MANAGER

SR. VICE PRESIDENT

SR. MANAGER

Figure 14.3

LEVEL 1: GET INSTRUCTIONS	LEVEL 2: RECOMMEND ACTIONS
The task should be performed according to a written and approved process instruction. The supervisor clearly sets deadlines and check-in points. Where a written and approved process instruction does not exist (a new task), the supervisor also clearly defines the task and explains the role of the employee and the supervisor and whether the task requires a verbal or written report.	The employee is expected to develop possible solutions and recommend–and justify–the best one. The supervisor will review the possible solutions, test the quality of the recommendation, and then make the decision on how to implement it.

LEVEL 3: ACT & CHECK IN	LEVEL 4: ACT & INFORM
The employee and the supervisor are clear on how the employee will perform the task. The employee works independently, but the supervisor oversees the work during pre-determined check-in points. The supervisor course-corrects if problems are encountered that the employee did not see.	The employee and the supervisor are clear on how the employee will perform the task. The employee understands that this is his/her task and is fully accountable for its successful completion. The employee informs the supervisor if exceptions or unique problems are encountered, and if not, informs the supervisor when the task is complete.

	LVL 1 0-25%	LVL 2 25-50%	LVL 3 50-75%	LVL 4 75-100%
MANAGES THE DEPARTMENT				
Manage the accounts payable process				
Manage the payroll process				

Figure 14.4

Several years ago, I was showing a Career Flow™ to an up-and-coming employee working for a vendor. I explained how it is created and how it is used. The more I explained, the quieter this person became.

Finally, I asked if they were confused or just didn't like the concept. They responded, "I wish my company had something like this, because I don't see a path forward right now, and no one is explaining my options." It wasn't long after that discussion that this person left that firm for another opportunity where they could see a career path for themselves.

Don't let this happen to you.

POSITION DESCRIPTIONS (WHAT I MUST DO)

Everyone hates writing position descriptions, and this is primarily because they are trying to write *one* document to facilitate *two* very different processes: hiring and assessing performance.

To facilitate the hiring process, organizations need a document that clearly communicates what employees in the position *do*, not what they need to *know*. Job applicants want to know what their typical day or week looks like, and organizations need to show them that without obfuscating.

Many position descriptions list a litany of responsibilities, most of which the employee will rarely, if ever, perform. This laundry list approach leads employees to invariably choose the items from the list that they like the best, thereby framing the position according to their own imagined version of the job.

By incorporating the use of process diagrams and Career Flows™, an organization can limit the use of position descriptions to the hiring process. A simple one-page document can be created that conveys the role the position serves in the department (or the organization) and the primary responsibilities assigned to that role.

It is also helpful to communicate how time is typically allocated among the various primary responsibilities of the position. This can be shown as a percentage of a typical day, week, or month depending on the position. This approach provides greater clarity to potential employees regarding what their typical work experience will be.

Technical Role
The GIS Analyst directs field operations and primarily completes technical tasks associated with geospatial surface analysis, designing, testing, and optimizing enterprise/multi-user databases, configuring and deploying ArcGIS Online applications. Technical tasks are assigned and overseen by Project Managers, and overhead tasks are assigned and overseen by the Service Area Manager.

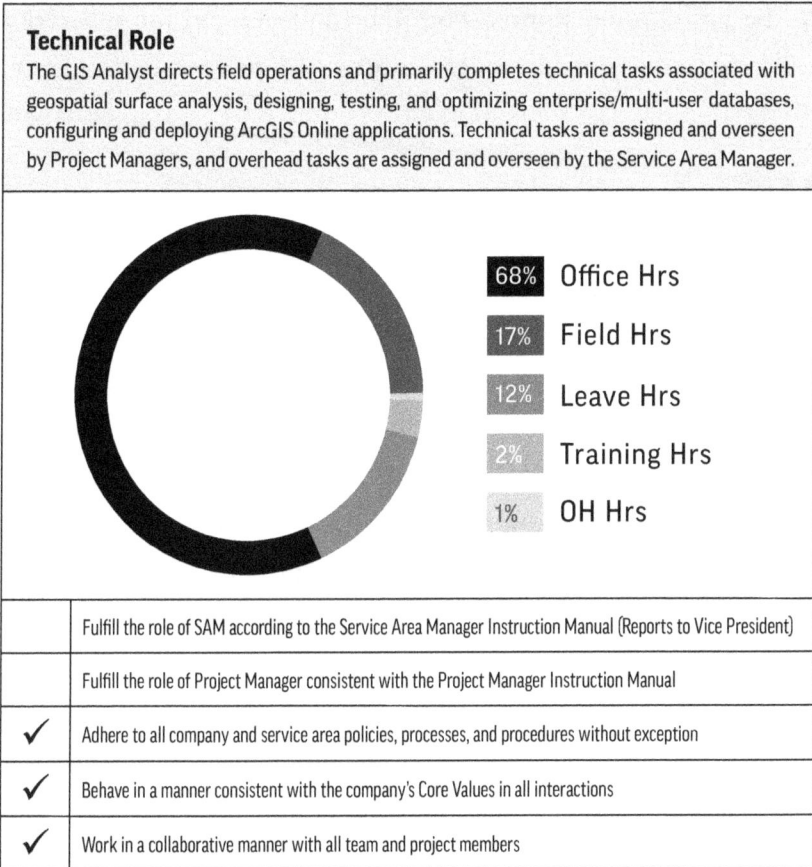

68%	Office Hrs
17%	Field Hrs
12%	Leave Hrs
2%	Training Hrs
1%	OH Hrs

	Fulfill the role of SAM according to the Service Area Manager Instruction Manual (Reports to Vice President)
	Fulfill the role of Project Manager consistent with the Project Manager Instruction Manual
✓	Adhere to all company and service area policies, processes, and procedures without exception
✓	Behave in a manner consistent with the company's Core Values in all interactions
✓	Work in a collaborative manner with all team and project members

Figure 14.5

Once hired, these time allocations help employees prioritize their efforts, preventing them from spending more (or less) time than is appropriate for a given primary responsibility and possibly short-changing other primary responsibilities.

Without a time allocation for primary responsibilities, supervisors can be challenged when assessing performance because the employee may be fulfilling one primary responsibility very well (what the *employee* will undoubtedly focus on) but not fulfilling another (what the *supervisor* may focus on). By adding a time allocation component to the position description, both the employee and the supervisor will be forced to use the same measuring stick to assess performance.

Motivation Turbocharger 2: Professional Development Plans

Career Flows™ are professional development plans that lay out the skills and knowledge each position needs and how to progress within and between positions by accumulating those skills and knowledge. Their use eliminates the aspect of performance assessments that employees and supervisors both hate—ambiguity. In addition, their use can facilitate the creation of thoughtful professional development plans tailored to each employee. By defining the skills that must be mastered in each position, and the progression of this mastery, a comprehensive professional development matrix showing the best way for employees to master each required skill can be simply developed.

These professional development training matrices help both supervisors and employees set realistic, shared goals for areas of skill mastery that can be pursued through work, mentoring, classes, or workshops. Rather than imposing a generic "training" program on your employees, wouldn't you prefer to supercharge their intrinsic motivation to advance and grow?

Motivation Turbocharger 3: Performance-Based Accountability

If you want to harness the power of your optimized Purpose, Strategy, Structure, Processes, and Core Values in your organization, you'll want to incorporate them into a *performance-based accountability program.*

By doing so, you effectively show employees how vital these fundamental elements are to the success of your organization, and the direct
impact their conduct and behaviors (whether positive or negative)
have on the success of your organization.

To make this impact perfectly clear, the approach to performance
assessments must be holistic, where the assessment considers not only
whether assigned responsibilities were fulfilled but also how *successfully*
they were fulfilled.

A good balance in the assessment is achieved when the employee's
conduct represents 50 percent of the performance assessment score
(the 'what' component) and the employee's *behaviors* represent the
remaining 50 percent (the 'how' component), of which one half is
assessed as adherence to your Rules, Policies, Processes, and Procedures and the other half as adherence to your Core Values.

PERFORMANCE ASSESSMENT

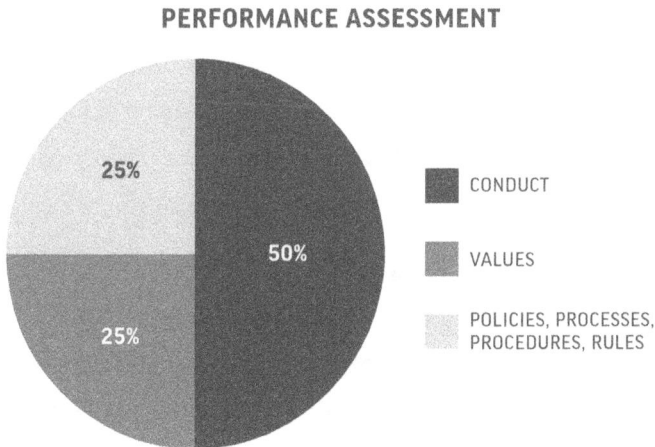

Figure 14.6

For the performance assessment to serve as an effective incentive
for employees to align their conduct and behaviors with the organization's objectives, particularly its risk management objectives, it
is important that all decisions regarding assignments, promotions,

professional development opportunities, and variable compensation consider performance assessment scores.

Motivation Turbocharger 4: Efforts-Based Rewards

Employees, in general, have far more control over what they put into their work (inputs) than they do the results of their work (outputs). Therefore, if you are going to use an extrinsic motivator like a rewards program (bonus plan, profit-sharing plan), it will be far more effective if the rewards are tied to employee efforts, not outcomes. And, if you are rewarding effort, your program should be designed such that *all* employees are eligible to participate in the plan rather than just a select few (e.g., sales staff, executive management). The key to avoiding the resentments created in the "everyone gets a bonus" type of plan, where top performers and laggards are rewarded equally, is a requirement that each employee *qualify* individually to receive a reward. This is easily accomplished by determining a minimum performance score that all employees must earn to qualify to share in the reward.

Your Culture is optimized when your Purpose, Strategy, Structure, and Processes are optimized, the incentives you use are closely tailored to this design, and incentives are tied to the behaviors of your employees (inputs) rather than results (outputs) they generate.

**Even if you are
on the right track,
you'll get run over
if you just sit there.**

———

WILL ROGERS

Conclusion

Now let's review what the fundamental components of the Sprocket design will look like in your organization, once you have completed the steps outlined in chapters 10–14.

- Your *Purpose* will set a clear destination for your organization.
- Your *Strategy* will leave your competitors in the rearview mirror.
- Your *Structure* will create a comfortable ride.
- Your *Processes* will have all pistons firing.
- Your *Culture* will easily allow you to travel over any terrain.

In essence, you will be driving your organization forward, with conviction.

You now have the knowledge necessary to redesign your business to be more successful and more prepared for the transformational changes that will be required of it. Whether the journey ahead for you is a short one or a long one, I promise it will be worth it.

Additional Resources

Sprocket Help

This book provided you with all the how-to information needed to optimize your organization using the Sprocket design.

If you are not the DIY type, and prefer a Done-for-Me option, you may be interested in our online Sprocket Assessment tool.

Sprocket®

Driving Your Business Forward

The online program allows several people from your organization to anonymously answer questions about how well each component of the Sprocket design is working in your organization. We compile the aggregate results and provide you with your Sprocket Adaptive Response Score, indicating the degree of imbalance in your business and which component(s) is (are) creating the imbalance. This "big picture" analysis typically results in a better understanding of those chronic problems that never seem to get resolved but are endlessly discussed.

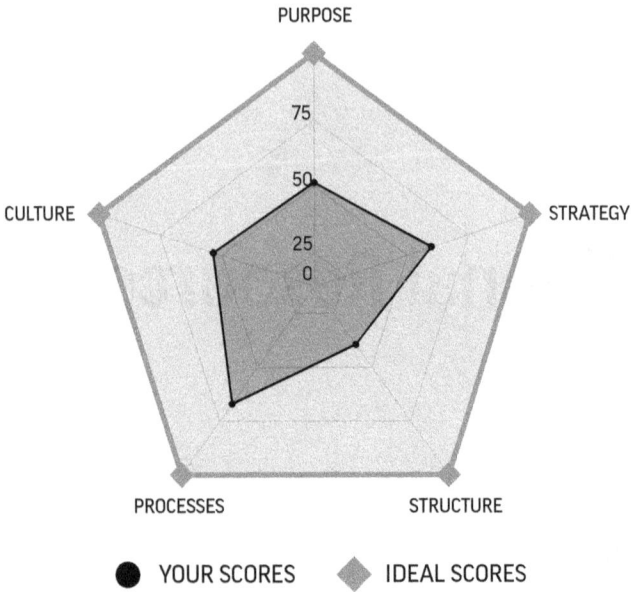

PURPOSE

75

50

25

0

CULTURE
STRATEGY

PROCESSES
STRUCTURE

● YOUR SCORES   ◆ IDEAL SCORES

Your Sprocket Purpose Score

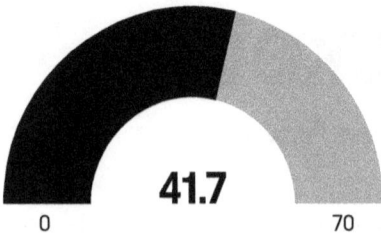

41.7

0   70

Our Staff Understands Our Business Purpose

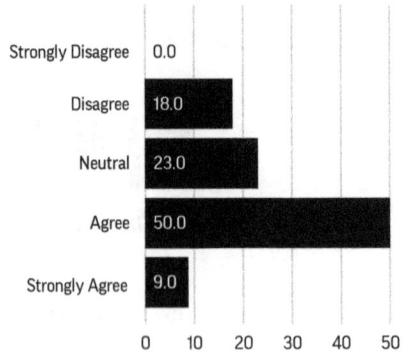

Strongly Disagree	0.0
Disagree	18.0
Neutral	23.0
Agree	50.0
Strongly Agree	9.0

0   10   20   30   40   50

After the first overall assessment, there is an optional assessment for each of the five components, where we dig deeper to root out the barriers that are holding you back.

If you want a guide who already has a good road map and knows all the shortcuts to be taken and the roadblocks to avoid, we can recommend certified trainers who can guide your team through the process.

America's Commerce Corps

Several years ago, when I was named a Small Business Person of the Year, the awards ceremony was held a few days before Memorial Day. It struck me that as a nation, we show appreciation for the groups that make our country what it is, be that the military, first responders, teachers, medical professionals, and so on. But *my* group—local business owners—was rarely shown appreciation for the contributions it makes to the country. This group had no collective identity; it didn't even have a name!

I corrected that oversight by coming up with a name befitting the role of local businesses in our country—America's Commerce Corps. This evolved into a grassroots program committed to strengthening communities across America by growing local economies. We are a community-based program of residents, businesses, nonprofits, and public agencies supporting one another economically with the shared goal of making the communities where we live and work vibrant, robust, and resilient for this generation and those to follow.

Sprocket is one tool offered in the America's Commerce Corps program. You can learn more about the program and the other tools offered to local organizations by visiting our website at www.americascommercecorps.org.

LOCAL BUSINESSES
STRENGTHENING COMMUNITIES